FANS
FRIENDS&
FOLLOWERS

BY SCOTT KIRSNER

First Edition
© 2009 Scott Kirsner / CinemaTech Books
Web site: http://www.scottkirsner.com/fff

Cover design by Matt W. Moore.

Photo credits: Tobin Poppenberg (DJ Spooky), Dale May (Jonathan
Coulton), JD Lasica (Gregg and Evan Spiridellis), Scott
Beale/LaughingSquid.com (Ze Frank), Dusan Reljin (OK Go), Todd
Swidler (Sarah Mlynowski). Tracy White and Dave Kellett provided their
own illustrations.

Printed and bound in the United States of America

10 9 8 7 6 5 4 3 2 1

Contents

Understanding the New Rules   I

Table: Defining the Terms   35

Introduction to the Interviews   36

Film & Video

Michael Buckley: Creator of "What the Buck"   37

Mike Chapman: Animator and Writer, "Homestar Runner"   41

Ze Frank: Multimedia Artist and Creator of "theshow"   45

Curt Ellis: Documentary Producer and Writer   52

Michael "Burnie" Burns: Creator of "Red vs. Blue"   56

Sandi DuBowski: Documentary Filmmaker   59

Gregg and Evan Spiridellis: Co-Founders, JibJab Media   62

Timo Vuorensola: Science Fiction Director   68

Steve Garfield: Videoblogger   71

Robert Greenwald: Documentary Filmmaker   73

M dot Strange: Animator   77

Music

Jonathan Coulton: Singer-Songwriter   81

Damian Kulash: Singer and Guitarist, OK Go   86

DJ Spooky: Composer, Writer and Multimedia Artist — 92

Jill Sobule: Singer-Songwriter — 95

Richard Cheese: Singer — 100

Chance: Singer-Songwriter — 104

Brian Ibbott: Host of the Podcast "Coverville" — 108

Visual Arts

Natasha Wescoat: Painter, Designer and Illustrator — 111

Tracy White: Comics Artist — 114

Matt W. Moore: Artist and Graphic Designer — 117

Dave Kellett: Comics Artist — 120

Dylan Meconis: Graphic Novelist — 124

Writing

Sarah Mlynowski: Novelist — 127

Brunonia Barry: Novelist — 131

Lisa Genova: Novelist — 134

Kris Holloway: Non-Fiction Author — 139

Comedy & Magic

Eugene Mirman: Comedian and Writer — 142

Dan and Dave Buck: Pioneers of Extreme Card Manipulation — 146

Mark Day: Comedian and YouTube Executive — 150

Exploring the New Business Models   154

Power Tools for Audience-Building, Collaboration
and Commerce   162

Supplemental Reading   176

Acknowledgments   179

About the Author   180

The Web Site   181

Understanding the New Rules: Building an Audience and a Creative Career in the Digital Age

Ernest Hemingway had Scribner's, his dependable publishing house.

Paul Cezanne had Ambroise Vollard to sell his paintings, and Georgia O'Keeffe had Alfred Stieglitz.

Francis Ford Coppola had Paramount Pictures.

Stevie Wonder had Motown, and the The Who had Warner Bros.

For the past century or two, artists have relied upon others to advance their careers: publishers, art dealers, movie studios, and record labels.

These businesses discovered new talent, and often had a hand in shaping its creative output. They cultivated an audience for the work, and they sold it – all while passing on some of the profits to the creator (in the best-case scenario, at least), so she could record another album or paint another landscape.

That system worked wonderfully for some artists. They could focus on their art without being distracted by business concerns. As they became more famous, they attained more creative control, and their work sold in large enough quantities that they tended not to worry much about the split – the share of revenue that their studio or publisher was taking from the price of every ticket or paperback sold.

Besides, there was no alternative: to have a really significant career, and reach a really wide audience, artists needed the system.

But now, its engine is wheezing and the gears are jamming. The machine just doesn't work the way it once did.

Record labels and movie studios don't dedicate the energy they once did to discovering and developing new talent - the next Beatles or Spielberg. (And when they do introduce a new band or filmmaker, they often abandon them after the inevitable first flop.) Their deep pockets don't give them an insurmountable marketing advantage in a world where blogs, YouTube videos, and Facebook can be incredibly effective in building a fan base, virtually for free. Finally, they no longer control the terrain where purchases take place, like the shelves of the local record store, video store, or bookstore. Consumers increasingly seem to be gravitating towards online retailers like Amazon.com, Etsy, Amie Street, and iTunes, which are open to independent creators in ways that the aisles of Blockbuster or Borders never were.

> "There has never been a noisier, more competitive time to try to make art, entertain people, and tell stories."

We've entered into what I call the era of digital creativity. In this era, artists have the tools to make anything they can envision, inexpensively. (I use the term "artist" to encompass everyone involved in a creative endeavor, from cartoonists to comedians to filmmakers to prestidigitators.) They can build teams and collaborate across great distances, bridging divides of language and culture. They can cultivate an audience and communicate with it regularly, carrying it (or at least a segment of it) with them from one project to another. And they can take control over the transaction, whether it is selling a work of art on eBay, a book through Amazon, or a ticket to a live performance via Brown Paper Tickets.

If you are a glass-half-full type, you've already realized that the era of digital creativity presents incredible opportunities. You can do what you love, reach an audience, and earn some money. What starts off as a small fan base can quite suddenly go global, enabling you to quit your day job and earn a solid living.

The flip side is that there has never been a noisier, more competitive time to try to make art, entertain people, and tell stories. Everyone is doing it, and so there is an incredible surplus of content in every art form.

In 2000, 973 full-length films were submitted to the Sundance Film Festival, generally considered the best platform for launching a new indie movie. By 2008, that number had risen to 3,624. (Just 121 were accepted.)

Think about a band trying to build a reputation in Los Angeles, a city with about 50 FM radio stations – and perhaps just three or four that matter in any particular genre (like Latino music, hip hop, or rock.) Now think about trying to build a reputation online. A link to the band's MySpace page from any one of several hundred well-regarded music blogs might result in a sold-out show. A song included in any of the thousands of podcasts that are distributed through iTunes might catch fire.

Breaking out, somehow, is both more of a possibility than it has ever been – and harder than it has ever been.

The attention of an individual audience member anywhere in the world is simultaneously easier to snare (a multi-million-dollar marketing campaign is no longer required) – and harder than ever to snare.

I wanted to write this book to share some of the ways that artists are grappling with those paradoxes.

In conversations over the past three years, I've been asking questions about how artists are attracting audiences and building careers in the online world.

I've found that many artists just want to keep doing things the old way: schmoozing and entering competitions and hanging out at Schwab's Drug Store, hoping to get discovered. Getting discovered, of course, will lead directly to the big deal with the big advance and the worldwide promotional tour.

It'll still happen, occasionally. But I think the odds are getting longer by the minute.

A small cadre of artists is taking a different tack. They've become convinced that the old power players – studios, record labels, publishers and the like – can no longer create and sustain individuals' careers the way they once did. So they're taking responsibility for building their reputation, telling their story, and assembling a fan base that can support them financially. They are experimenting with new ways to finance their work, promote it, and sell it. They're creating new connections between themselves and their audience. They're exploring new genres in which to work, and releasing their work in new ways and at different tempos. (Why should fans wait eighteen months between albums, or three years between novels?)

Yes, it's a lot of work to build a career in the era of digital creativity. But there are huge benefits. You no longer need to sell an editor or A&R rep on your artistic vision before you can start writing or recording. Your publisher can't drop you, and you won't sink into a depression when your label goes under. The on-going conversation with your audience can be a source of inspiration, motivation, and ideas.

It's this powerful new link with the audience that the old power players don't understand. They still live in a world of press releases, flashy billboards in Times Square, and expensive-but-never-changing Web sites.

> "It's this powerful new link with the audience that the old power players don't understand."

And many established artists with a few successes on their résumé are happy to have other people worry about dealing with the audience. "Let the publicity department schedule my press tour, and the marketing department handle those billboard buys," they think. "I'm going to focus on my creative process." That approach can be effective. It's expensive, of course – but who cares, if someone else is footing the bill? The danger is that it's too easy for artists to lose touch with the audience if they don't have any sort of on-going connection with the people supporting their work.

In this new era, artists like the musician Jill Sobule, the animator M dot Strange, the cartoonist Tracy White, the YouTube personality Michael Buckley, and the comedian Eugene Mirman have been among the pioneers in understanding the power of a new kind of relationship with the audience. This new digital audience wants to participate and collaborate; get a glimpse of your creative process and learn from you; vote and comment; and help spread the word about your latest project. They may even be willing to help fund your next endeavor.

But a word of warning: unlike pretending to be fond of your Uncle Larry at Thanksgiving dinner, this relationship with your audience cannot be faked.

The very term "audience" may be on its way to obsolescence. Some artists prefer to think of themselves as cultivating a "community," attracting "supporters," or organizing and motivating a "street team." Some like the term "fan base," while others may choose to use the terms "collaborators" or "co-conspirators." That's up to you. But what seems to be emerging as a constant in this new era is that a large chunk of the audience will remain passive consumers of the work you create – people who buy tickets or DVDs or merchandise, and that's it. A much smaller percentage (perhaps five or ten percent, or, if you're lucky, twenty) will want to be more engaged, helping spread the gospel to others or participating in the creative process, for instance. Many of the forward-thinking artists I've interviewed have spent a lot of time brainstorming about how to get that more active segment of their audience involved, or simply *listening* to them explain how *they* would like to be involved.

Understanding this new relationship, I think, is going to be crucial to success in the era of digital creativity. It is the foundation upon which careers will be built.

The people I sought out for this book are all at working at the vanguard of these changes. They've been among the first to start to understand how to bring together a community in this new era ... how to maintain a tight relationship with that community ... and how to leverage that community's support to produce new kinds of work and make a living at it.

For the most part, they're artists who've launched their careers online – rather than people who started out with the backing of a movie studio or publisher, and then began to discover the merits of communicating with their fans on the Internet. They represent the full gamut of technological literacy, from people who can write their own software (like the musician Jonathan Coulton, who once worked as a programmer) to people who rely on friends or fans or hired hands to set up and maintain their Web sites.

Over the course of dozens of conversations (many of which are included or excerpted here), a set of successful strategies and tactics started to emerge – things that were particularly effective in attracting an audience and contributing to an artist's economic self-sufficiency. These are by no means the only strategies that will work. People are pioneering new approaches daily, and you may well discover something that works for you that no one has thought to try before.

> Be Remarkable, and Make Remarkable Stuff

In the crowded and noisy party that is the Internet, you don't want to wear what everyone else is wearing.

Be different. Create work only you can create. Since there are no gatekeepers, there's no one to tell you that your art or music or video is unmarketable, too weird, too challenging.

Sometimes, being remarkable can mean being topical and timely, like the jaunty political satires and year-in-review animations produced by JibJab Media. The Internet loves to talk about what's happening *now*. Sometimes, being remarkable entails being provocative: saying something that no one else is saying.

Being remarkable can be about doing something you're not supposed to do. Improv Everywhere stages unusual and humorous "missions" in public places – like riding the subway without pants, or shopping at a Home Depot in slow-motion – and then posts the resulting videos online. (They've so far released three DVDs that capture their 80-plus missions, along with bonus material.)

Sometimes, being remarkable involves giving people something to talk about, a handle, a reason to share or blog about what you're doing. One of the things that helped make Bon Iver's debut album, "For Emma, Forever Ago," a success was the back-story that came with it. After breaking up with his girlfriend (and the band he'd been part of), songwriter Justin Vernon went to a remote hunting cabin in northern Wisconsin to record a new album. He posted the songs to his MySpace page, burned 500 CDs, and sent a few to music bloggers in the hopes of getting some reviews. Before long, blogs like Pitchfork were buzzing about the songs, and Vernon was appearing on "Letterman," signing with a record label, and playing sold-out shows. "A big part of Mr. Vernon's success...was crafting a compelling story to help fans connect to the music even more," the Wall

Street *Journal* explained. "Bon Iver's MySpace page, Web site and CD all include the same story: a paragraph telling how Mr. Vernon wrote the songs while hibernating in the remote cabin in the woods."

One of the secrets to succeeding in the era of digital creativity is doing something different, and then finding ways to share it with people who might appreciate it. At first, you may feel as though you're connecting only with tiny, disparate, niche audiences, but if enough niche audiences discover and support your work, you'll soon have something truly substantial.

> Create Opportunities for Participation

Online, a significant segment of the audience no longer wants to just consume. They want to collaborate. That collaboration can take many forms, from voting on their favorite book cover design to sending in their own photos to be used as part of a giant photo mural.

The documentary filmmaker Robert Greenwald has both asked supporters to make small donations so that he could complete a film about Iraq (he wound up raising more than

> "Sometimes, the audience will explain to you how they'd like to be involved."

$200,000) and also relied on some of his more active collaborators for help with research and even shooting interviews. Jonathan Coulton, the Brooklyn-based musician, held a competition on his blog to find the best fan-submitted solo to fill a break he'd left in a song called "Shop Vac."

Part of this desire to participate is driven by the fact that everyone on the Internet craves recognition and connection. Part of it is driven by the fact that many of your followers are trying to establish their own careers as writers, artists, filmmakers.

Sometimes, the audience will explain to you how they'd like to be involved. When the band OK Go made a hit YouTube video that featured the four members doing an elaborately-choreographed dance routine in a backyard, fans started sending in videos of themselves aping the routine. The band started posting them on its Web site, and then created a formal contest with trophies and a grand prize to keep the momentum going. (The winners were flown to an OK Go concert to dance onstage with the band, and many of the entrants were shown on various TV shows, including "The Colbert Report.")

Some new-era creators choose to serve as ringleaders, and let their community take on much of the creative heavy-lifting. Timo Vuorensola, the Finnish director of *Star Wreck* and the forthcoming *Iron Sky*, has solicited comments on scripts from the Internet community; found actors online; enlisted the help of volunteer special effects experts; sought musicians to write the score; and received help translating the film into roughly 30 different languages. "*Star Wreck* was made by a core crew of five people," he says, "and over 300 people are credited in the end credits, and a community of 3000 people were more or less involved in making it."

Filmmakers like Richard Linklater and Brett Gaylor have given their followers footage to play with. In Linklater's case, he invited people to create their own version of a promotional trailer for his movie *A Scanner Darkly*. Gaylor asked visitors to OpenSourceCinema.org to contribute photos and videos related to Girltalk, the musician who is the subject of his documentary "RiP: A Remix Manifesto." Gaylor also encouraged site visitors to remix the raw footage he'd shot. (Worth watching is the animated remix created by students at Concordia University, at http://www.opensourcecinema.org/node/2178.) In both cases, this strategy ensured that many different versions or fragments of the film spread around the Internet, helping to increase awareness.

As an artist, you may have a bit of reflexive hostility toward the idea of letting your fans elbow their way into your creative process. But it's worth trying at least a small experiment to see how it changes your relationship with your fans, and their relationship with you. Perhaps the experiment will involve helping select the rough demo you'll turn into a finished single, or inviting fans to suggest locations where you might shoot the first-date scene in your screenplay. Often, your community will jump at the chance to help you solve logistical problems; when cartoonist Dave Kellett has traveled the country on book tours, his readers have occasionally offered to accept shipments of his latest book, and transport them to the site of an event.

Whatever they do, be sure thank them publicly on your site, or credit them in the finished work.

The more opportunities you create for fans to participate in your process, the more engaged and loyal you'll find they become. They'll step up to be a financier, PR agent, tour coordinator, copy editor, Web site designer, or second-unit cameraman. Managing all these collaborators can get complex. But their investment of time and energy will free you up to do more of the work you want to do, and they'll help spread the gospel in a way you can hardly imagine.

> Understand the Power of the Link

Chasing coverage in traditional media can be exhausting, with or without a full-time PR person on the payroll. Imagine all the work that goes into securing an author appearance on "Fresh Air with Terry Gross," or trying to get your band booked on "Saturday Night Live."

Even if you succeed, think about what happens in the audience member's mind. They may enjoy your music. They may even remember the name of the band. The next time they're perusing the iTunes Store, or shopping at the mall, they need to remember that they liked your stuff, recall your name, and make the purchase. That initial spark of interest needs to be rekindled – days, weeks, or months later. A tiny percentage of the audience that saw your performance on TV will ever actually consummate a purchase.

> "A tiny percentage of the audience that saw your performance on TV will ever actually consummate a purchase."

While you should certainly grab national media exposure if and when you can get it, there's incredible power in online media coverage, specifically because the blog reader or podcast listener who gets exposed to your work is much closer to actually buying something. They're on their computer already. The blog may link directly to an online storefront like Amazon or iTunes; even if it links to your site, you have a prominent "Buy" button awaiting visitors (don't you?)

If a site writes about you but doesn't include a link, by all means you should get in touch and request one. Most online publishers will happily comply – but you will be surprised how stubborn the Web sites of many traditional magazines and newspapers can be about including one little link.

It's also worth monitoring the way people wind up at your site. If you run your own Web site or blog, you can easily get statistics software from your hosting company, or from a free service like SiteMeter, that will show you where visitors are coming from. Google Analytics, a free service, is another great option for gathering this data. Looking at this "referral data" – a long list of sites that referred or pointed people to you – will show you which online coverage is actually paying off with additional traffic. (With social networks like MySpace and Facebook, this kind of visitor tracking is just about impossible.) If your commerce vendor supports it, you may also offer certain sites a special discount code ("10 percent off if you enter the code XYZ.") That allows you to see which sites are actually driving the most purchases, based on how often a given code is used.

All links are powerful, but some are more powerful than others. The tech culture blog Boing Boing is famous for sending so much traffic to sites it covers that many of them temporarily collapse under the weight of all those unexpected visitors. When you discover a particular site or blogger that generates a lot of traffic and purchase activity for you, put them at the top of your media outreach list. Offer them exclusive photos from your next movie shoot, or an outtake from your forthcoming album, or an exclusive excerpt from your next book. Give them reasons to keep covering you – and linking to you.

The most powerful link of all, by most people's measures, is the link to your site from Google. When people type in your name, or the title of your latest project, your official site ought to show up as the first result, or at least on the first page. You can certainly find much better advice about "search engine marketing" than mine, but there are a few key tenets. (Search engine marketing is an entire field focused on helping sites ensure that they appear prominently in lists of search engine results.)

First is that you want people who have Web sites that are more popular than yours, and who've been running them for a while, to link to you. That gives you cred, in the eye's of Google's software algorithm. Second, if your site is composed entirely of graphics, video, and nifty Flash animations, but light on text, there won't be much to help Google understand who you are. A bio, a list of all your books (or albums, or movies), and a description of the genres/forms you work in are all helpful to have on your site. Third, the longer your site has been up, and the more frequently you update it, the more likely it is to be regarded highly by Google. (See the Reading List at the end of the book for two links related to improving your Google ranking.)

One free tool that can be helpful in figuring out how well-designed your site is, from the perspective of enticing search engines to link to it, is Website Grader (http://website.grader.com).

Accumulating links from lots of little online communities that most people have never heard of is not quite as glamorous as landing a spot on "The Today Show." But the traffic and purchases you'll get from those direct links can add up to impressive levels.

And if you do wind up on "The Today Show," be sure you take a moment to mention your Web site, or MySpace profile, or Facebook presence. It can't hurt – even if most people won't remember it.

> Don't Be Reluctant to Ask for a Review or Rating

One sure-fire way to expand your audience is through positive reviews, ratings, and other endorsements of your work. These can range from a four-star rating of your latest album on iTunes, a two-line review of your book on Amazon, or a rave about last night's performance on a blog dedicated to stand up comedy.

Sometimes, reviews will just pop up organically, the result of fans checking out your latest work and taking matters in their own hands.

> "Often, a little nudge is necessary to trigger an avalanche of positive write-ups."

But often, a little nudge is necessary to trigger an avalanche of positive write-ups – especially early in your career. Many of YouTube's top personalities figured this out, and began openly requesting that their viewers rate a video, post a comment, or subscribe to their channel, all of which helped expand their audience.

If you're releasing an important new project, send advance copies to mentors, influential bloggers, and people whose opinion you respect. (Some people will be OK if you send along a digital copy or point them to a URL where they can download the work, but others will prefer receiving a physical copy in the old-fashioned US mail.) Include a note that mentions the release date, and requests a review on the recipient's blog, or a "blurb"/endorsement that you can use on your site.

When I was preparing to release my last book, *Inventing the Movies*, I sent out about 20 advance copies in the mail. They went to people who'd helped me with the project, people who might review it, and well-known people in the entertainment and media businesses who I thought would be willing to provide a blurb that would lend the book credibility. About 15 went to people I knew, and five went to newspaper book review sections or people I had no real connection to. Once people had a couple weeks to read (or skim) the book, I e-mailed to follow up. With some people, I asked them for a blurb that I'd use on the book's Web site. With others, I waited until the book showed up on Amazon.com, and asked them to post a review there.

I also made sure to include my e-mail address in the book, and on the book's Web site. Whenever a reader e-mailed me a positive comment, I thanked them – and asked nicely to see whether they'd mind also posting their comments on Amazon.

My campaign was far from perfect, but it generated about a dozen blurbs for my site, a dozen reviews on Amazon, and a five-star rating on that site. (I tried to contain my anger toward one friend and one random book buyer who doled out just four stars.)

The objective should be that wherever your work is sold, there are at least a handful of good reviews and ratings. I don't recommend trying to game the system (by posting your own pseudonymous reviews, for instance), but you should encourage friends and fans to make their opinions heard all over the Internet. Those first few reviews will make others feel more inclined to post their own thoughts. And reading kind words about your work will help persuade that new fan to make a purchase.

> Choose the Platforms You're Going to Use

Online, there are countless platforms you can use to distribute your work and stay in touch with your audience, from Facebook to Twitter, Blogger to MySpace, YouTube to e-mails.

Some exceptionally experimental artists will enjoy trying out every new platform that comes along, from Twittering on their iPhone (publishing short messages to a group of "followers") to broadcasting live video from a camera built into their hat.

It's easy to get overwhelmed and distracted by every new technology that pops up. But it's also not necessary to have more than one solid place where fans can find your work and keep up with your career.

If you're intimidated by the prospect of setting up your own Web site right now, or you want to do something quickly, it's easy to set up a blog using free (or cheap) services like TypePad or Blogger, set up an account on YouTube where you can upload videos, or create a profile on MySpace.

Start in one place, and focus on promoting that destination (and letting people discover it) before you expand to something else.

When you're out and about, performing shows or schmoozing at conferences or appearing on TV, focus for a while on plugging that first platform, rather than mentioning several places where people can find your work ("Look for us on Facebook" or "You can find the trailer and a bunch of scenes at YouTube...be sure to leave a comment or a rating!")

> "The best platform is your own Web site with your own Web address, since that gives you the most control over how you look."

The best platform, of course, is your own Web site with your own Web address, since that will be most memorable to prospective fans, and it gives you the most control over how you look - and how you sell your work. Your own site can be a gateway, directing fans to another site where you may be a guest blogger, or a podcast where your band is featured, for instance. You'll also have more insight into who's visiting your site, where they're coming from, and what they're doing, since Web hosting services usually offer free statistics and analysis packages, while social networking sites like Facebook only keep track of how many friends you've got.

Building a Web site doesn't need to be expensive. You can ask artists you respect who built their sites (and how much it cost, and how long it took.) You can advertise on Craigslist, or find freelancers on sites like Elance or

Guru.com. Your city likely has an art school that teaches Web design, and students are often eager to do *pro bono* work to build up their portfolios.

One thing that's very important to consider as you're building your site is how it will be updated. It's a bad idea to depend on the original designer to make every modification; you (or a member of your team) should be able to update your own appearance calendar, add new text to the homepage, etc.

A few people manage to successfully flout this rule about choosing a few key platforms. They're so energetic and prolific that they can communicate to their audience through multiple channels, like a plate-spinner keeping eight plates in the air. Michael Buckley, the host of the YouTube show "What the Buck" is one example: he maintains a presence on YouTube, Twitter, Blog.tv (a live video streaming site), MySpace, and Facebook.

But for most people, a tight focus on one or two platforms will work best.

> Find Your Ideal Frequency

Building a strong relationship with your audience online requires some sort of regular, predictable pace of communication. Just as your relationship with your best friend would fade if you decided not to call, text, or e-mail for half a year, the same result will play out if you neglect your online community.

This isn't to say you need to force yourself to produce some new piece of artwork every day or week.

For some artists, yes, having this direct channel to the audience will inspire them to make a photograph every day, record a new song every week, or write a short story every month. But whatever your pace of production, you ought to look for opportunities to stay in touch with your audience while you're working – during those phases when you're hunting for inspiration, cranking out rough drafts, or polishing and editing.

That may entail posting a Flickr set of the photos you've taken in Venice while scouting locations for your next movie. It could involve a blog post about the vintage Martin guitar you've just found at a flea market, along with a quick MP3 that lets your fans hear what the instrument sounds like.

You might record audio or video from a Q&A session you've done while on tour for your latest book. Or you might offer an early look at character sketches from your next graphic novel.

Whatever platform or platforms you choose as a way to keep in touch with your fan base, you don't want to fall silent for months at a time. Interest will wane, or evaporate entirely. Experiment with different frequencies to find one that feels comfortable. You might let other members of your creative team chip in every once in a while, but don't delegate communications with your fans entirely.

> "You don't want to fall silent for months at a time. Interest will wane, or evaporate entirely."

And in between your own posts and contributions, encourage your fans to talk amongst themselves in discussion forums on your site, or by leaving comments on your blog.

❧ Your Audience is Already Hanging Out Somewhere

You could organically build your audience one by one, as people discover you and tell their friends. But why?

Many of the artists who've built truly large audiences have relied on lots of online and offline help.

It begins by giving thought to the types of people who seem to like your stuff. You might ask people at performances, gallery openings, or speaking gigs how they first found out about your work, or how they heard about this specific event. You might survey some of your fans to learn where else they hang out online, what their favorite blogs are for discovering new music, where they read reviews of new movies, etc. It could be that there's an especially well-read alternative weekly paper in your city that informs readers about shows and new releases, or that postings on the site Upcoming (http://upcoming.yahoo.com) let people know what's happening on any given Saturday night.

Start building a list of these sites and information sources, and open a channel of communication with them. Let them know about what you're up to, give their readers special discounts, or offer them exclusive content or "sneak peeks" of forthcoming work.

Documentarian Robert Greenwald began assembling his digital fan base through a partnership with the Democratic activist group MoveOn.org. Beginning with his 2004 release *Uncovered: The Truth About the Iraq War*, MoveOn let its membership list know about the film, offered DVDs for sale, and encouraged its members to organize their own house party screenings. Greenwald expected he might sell 2,000 copies of the DVD, but 120,000 copies were eventually sold. Other sites, like AlterNet and BuzzFlash, have also helped introduce people to Greenwald's documentaries, using them as premiums for fund-raising initiatives (for instance, a $30 donation to the site gets you a DVD.)

For musicians like Richard Cheese and Chance, exposure on popular podcasts like "Coverville" has helped beef up their fan bases. Writers like Sarah Mlynowksi report that one of the most effective things that brings her new readers is when another writer who shares a similar audience blogs about one of her books.

You may discover through your own research that there are a cluster of blogs on the topic of your latest film. Or you may learn by talking to their fans that many of them belong to a Facebook group for bluegrass music, or a mailing list for readers who are fond of historical fiction.

Be on the lookout for these places where your tribe-members spend time. Collect them in a Word document or a special bookmarks folder. Get to know the people who run them. And don't just view them as outlets for promotion – think about what you can give them and their audiences in return, and how you can let *your* fans know that *their* blog or e-mail list exists.

> Be Relentlessly Redundant About Your Web Site

This one's not particle physics: whatever you make, sell, or otherwise set adrift in the world should include your Web address. It ought to be in the credits of every video you make, in the liner notes of every CD, on the last page of every promotional PDF sample from your latest book. And explain to people what they'll get when they go to your site: "To download free live shows by the Incredible Edibles and see our latest tour schedule, visit www...." Or "To learn more about this issue, visit www...."

> Abide by the 15-Second Rule

A well-placed hook has never been more essential.

Exhibit A: Watch the YouTube video "Evolution of Dance," which for years now has been the most-popular user-generated video on the site (more than 100 million plays, and counting.) Notice that there's no prelude, aside from an announcer who intones the words "Evolution of Dance." The music starts (Elvis Presley's "Hound Dog,") and just before the 15-second point, the music changes (Chubby Checker's "The Twist"). Suddenly, you start to get the premise: this is going to be a fast-segueing survey of American dance styles.

The creator of "Evolution of Dance," Judson Laipply, may have intuitively understood that Internet audiences have extremely short attention spans – shorter, for sure, than radio listeners, ticket-buyers in movie theaters, or TV viewers with a remote control in

> "If you think about how quickly people surf around the Web, it's insane," says JibJab co-founder Gregg Spiridellis.

hand. He sought to hook you within the first 15 seconds, and give you a reason to keep watching.

On iTunes, prospective buyers of a song get to hear a 30-second sample. Jonathan Coulton's most popular song on iTunes, "Code Monkey," outlines the situation he's writing about (an underappreciated programmer toiling in a cubicle farm), gets in a quick joke, and has the guitars kick in before fifteen seconds have elapsed.

When JibJab Media produces one of their animated music videos, they strive to jam a joke into every line of the song, and there's a visual gag that accompanies each lyrical gag. "You want to hook your audience as soon as possible," says JibJab co-founder Gregg Spiridellis. "If you think about how quickly people surf around the Web, it's insane. Music is great to hook an audience quickly, and you have to tell jokes very quickly."

This isn't to say that you can't sustain people's attention over time – that no one will ever again read an epic fantasy novel, listen to a concept album in one sitting, or watch an engrossing two-hour documentary. But when someone is getting their first taste of your work, you need to give them a reason – quickly – to dive in deeper. What you're up to needs to be crystal clear, or so mysterious and bizarre that people can't help but have their curiosity piqued.

Think about your own Web surfing habits. It's hardly ever a focused, leisurely activity. Several windows are usually open at once. There's work waiting to be done in Word. E-mails chime as they arrive in your inbox. Chat windows pop up with friends looking to make plans. That fragmented attention is what makes the 15-Second Rule a rule.

Cut to the chase, and cut out any opening preliminaries. "Why would your video have opening credits?" asks comedian and YouTube executive Mark Day. "If your credits are thirty seconds long for a three-minute video, that's like have a ten-minute opening credit sequence for a half-hour sitcom."

You don't necessarily need to have a bomb go off every fifteen seconds in your film, or change the key of your song every eight bars. But you need to use those first fifteen seconds to amuse, seduce, surprise, or intrigue the person sampling your work before they're distracted by something else.

> Let Anyone Be Your Barnum

Circus founder P.T. Barnum was famous for his unflagging promotional skills. On the Internet, there are a million mini-Barnums who can help promote your career.

But you need to give them the right tools.

Just a few years ago, only "certified media outlets" were granted access to press kits and promotional materials. (Amazingly, there are still some movie studio and record label Web sites where you need to fill out a form or e-mail someone before you can get access to the press area.)

Now, anyone with a blog, podcast, live Internet video show, or Web site may want to talk about your work. Why not make it easy, supplying them with high-resolution photos, detailed bios, background info, and audio and video clips? (Of course, you should make yourself accessible, too, responding quickly to interview requests...or having a designated representative who will.) If a blogger or journalist requests something special for their coverage, like the story of what inspired you to make your latest film, add that to your online press kit.

You may want to offer some guidelines about how the material can be used – asking, for instance, that your photographer get credit, or that any publicity include a link to your site.

But it's crucial to make your press materials easily accessible, and easy to find on your site.

> Help People Learn to Do What You Do

One common thread among most creators who've attracted a large following online is that they are generous about sharing their knowledge. Some fraction of your audience wants to do exactly what you're doing, whether it's stand-up comedy, animation, or card tricks.

Burnie Burns, creator of the animated series "Red vs. Blue," posted an extensive FAQ about how others could use videogame consoles to produce their own animations, a genre called "machinima." (On his site, there's also a discussion forum where other machinima makers can share tips.) Jonathan Coulton wrote a blog post titled "How I Did It," talking about how he left his day job and laid the foundation for his musical career. Chance, another singer-songwriter, posts a "Geek Out" page for every single he records, listing the software, instruments, and microphones he employed. M dot Strange, who runs a one-man animation studio in San Jose, continually adds to a series of YouTube videos he calls "Film Skool," offering insight into how he works.

"I've found that educational stuff can attract an audience," he says. "Share your techniques, and tell people about the software you're using."

Dan and Dave Buck, siblings from Sonora, California who helped pioneer the genre of "flourishes," a kind of card manipulation that is part magic and part kinetic art, have built a business around educating others. They sell books, DVDs, and video-on-demand tutorials on their Web site. More than 10,000 people have purchased their three DVD box set, "The Trilogy" – for $85 a pop.

Whether or not you want to build a business around teaching others, positioning yourself as a knowledgeable expert in your field, especially if you're doing innovative things, will often generate media coverage. And the aspiring musicians, writers, or artists who benefit from the advice and tips you share will be far more likely to help spread the word about what you're doing.

> Don't Depend on the Bookmark

In the first few years of the Web's existence, lots of Web sites suggested that you bookmark them, and "come back often to see what's new."

Many people do have lists of bookmarked sites that they check regularly. But you can't depend on it.

Instead, you need to have a conduit to your audience that will allow you to communicate with them when you're doing something new, rather than waiting for them to migrate back to your site again.

One kind of conduit is an e-mail list that you maintain with a service like Constant Contact or Vertical Response, collecting e-mails on your site and then sending out bulletins when you've got a new product out or are announcing a tour. Another is an e-mail service like FeedBlitz, which allows people to subscribe to your blog by entering their e-mail, and receive an update whenever you've added new content.

But there's a sense that with an increase in e-mail traffic, everyone is paying a bit less attention to newsletters and other "shotgun"-style mass e-mails.

Setting up a Facebook fan page is another kind of conduit, since you can send messages to all the people who've declared themselves fans.

For more sophisticated users who are comfortable with RSS reader software, you'll likely want to offer an RSS feed of your blog using a free service like FeedBurner. (RSS stands for "Really Simple Syndication.")

That allows someone who is using Google Reader or My Yahoo, for instance, to "subscribe" to the latest content from your blog. RSS can also be a vehicle for publishing audio and video content, not just text.

Twitter is another conduit where people can sign up to follow you, opening a permanent (you hope) channel of communication.

For really urgent news – like a national TV or satellite radio appearance – you may want to use text messaging as a conduit, although sending text messages that are irrelevant to the recipient or too frequent can be annoying. Several fee-based services like Trumpia allow you to collect phone numbers from your fans and communicate via text.

> "You don't need more than one conduit that lets you communicate with your fan base. But having at least one is essential."

Some people choose to have multiple e-mail lists, or use a conduit like e-mail for a specific purpose. Author Sarah Mlynowski has one e-mail list for readers of her adult "chick lit" novels, and another for readers of her books for teens. Artist Natasha Wescoat uses Twitter and her blog for general news about what she's up to, but her e-mail list of about 500 people is geared primarily to buyers of her work. They find out about new artwork first, and receive discounts and free shipping. "I'm a little more personal on my e-mail list than my blog," she says. "The list is for people who are truly interested in my work, and want to watch my career."

You don't need to have more than one conduit that lets you communicate with your fan base. But having at least one is essential. You should promote it prominently on your Web site, explain what people will receive and how often they'll receive it ("I send out a weekly e-mail with a sneak peek of the film I'm currently working on"), and offer simple instructions about how to get connected ("To join my Facebook fan page...")

> Your Fan Database, and Geotagging It

You may opt not to use an e-mail list as one of your conduits to communicate with fans. That's up to you.

But e-mail is one medium that you control entirely (Facebook or MySpace, for instance, could decide tomorrow to unilaterally change their rules about how you communicate with fans and friends.) And even if people's alertness to new messages in their inboxes is on the wane, many artists still feel that a database of e-mail addresses is one of their most valuable assets. It's something that can call attention to new releases, live events, or funding campaigns, and it can reinforce things like blog entries, Twitter messages, or Facebook status updates. (See the "Power Tools" section of this book for a list of services that help collect e-mails and manage out-going messages.) If you ever choose to work with a big media company as a partner, bringing to the party your list of 10,000 or 100,000 e-mail addresses will likely get you a sweeter deal.

> "If you ever choose to work with a big media company, bringing to the party your list of e-mail addresses will likely get you a sweeter deal."

And if you ever plan to do live events, like concerts, film screenings, book readings, or gallery shows, consider asking your fans to give you some geographical info in addition to their e-mail. That will enable you to target messages just to fans who live around Chicago when you have an event there; it can be annoying for fans in Miami to hear about events they can't get to, and your Chicago area fans are much more likely to help you spread the word about the event, or assist you with logistics.

Fans who sign up for novelist Sarah Mlynowski's e-mail list input their city along with their e-mail address. The information goes into an Excel spreadsheet that Mlynowski can then sort, allowing her to e-mail fans in Los Angeles when she does a reading there.

Filmmakers Susan Buice and Arin Crumley got a bit more sophisticated, asking people interested in seeing their 2005 movie *Four Eyed Monsters* to share their ZIP code. That allowed Buice and Crumley to analyze the parts of the country where screenings of the film would attract the biggest audiences, and helped make those theatrical runs more profitable.

Tools for geotagging and geotargeting aren't yet very sophisticated; you may have to ask your Web site developer to build something custom, or use a rudimentary approach like Mlynowski's spreadsheet. But it can pay off, making your database of fan e-mail addresses even more valuable.

> Pay Attention to Behavioral Shifts, and Take Advantage of Them

What's a behavioral shift? Anything that represents a new way that your potential audience members are spending their time.

When TV started showing up in American living rooms in the late 1940s, and suddenly you didn't need to buy a movie ticket to consume visual entertainment, that was a behavioral shift. The arrival of VCRs in the 1970s represented another shift.

When the Web and e-mail emerged in the mid-1990s and suddenly people started spending time surfing Web sites and reading e-mail, that was a behavioral shift.

When MP3s and portable MP3 players came along, and then when Apple introduced the iPod in 2001, that was a behavioral shift. Suddenly, people could get music digitally and no longer *needed* to buy CDs to hear their favorite bands.

Same thing with the introduction of YouTube in 2005, and the arrival of e-book readers from Sony and Amazon a few years later. Video was suddenly easy to consume on the Internet, and books became easy to purchase and read in digital form.

Creators who pay attention to those behavioral shifts can build big audiences, very quickly. It's like riding a bobsled down a mountain instead of snow-shoeing up it.

Are all your friends suddenly setting up profiles on Facebook, and installing all kinds of "apps" on their profile? Passing around short, funny videos? Pay attention to these behavioral shifts, as they tend to create either new ways to communicate with your audience, new kinds of content for you to create (short videos instead of feature films, for instance), or new business opportunities.

In the 1950s, Walt Disney observed that Americans were suddenly buying TV sets and spending evenings in front of them. While the rest of Hollywood viewed television as a threat to their business of selling movie tickets, Disney started making shows and movies for television – and not only generated millions of dollars of new revenue, but also discovered that TV was a great way to promote his theatrical releases like *20,000 Leagues Under the Sea* and his new theme parks. The other movie studios rushed to play catch-up, making their own content for TV.

If you were paying attention in the 1990s, you noticed that teenagers were spending an increasing amount of money on videogame consoles, portable gaming devices, and game software. Then, massively multi-player online role-playing games (MMPORGs is the unwieldy acronym) like Ultima Online and World of Warcraft started attracting millions of players, each of whom paid a monthly subscription fee to design their own characters and go on quests. Those trends created new creative and business opportunities for anyone who wanted to tell stories or create virtual environments that would appeal to this vast population of gamers.

> "Pay attention to these behavioral shifts in how people communicate and consume."

Hundreds of musicians took advantage of the arrival of the MP3 format to either give away music for free (and spark additional CD sales) or sell it as a digital download; a few, like Metallica and the Beatles, chose to stay on the sidelines and ignore this behavioral shift.

When big media companies ignored the arrival of YouTube and iTunes (and other sites that made it easy to publish, share, and purchase video), people simply posted popular content anyway, whether it was on YouTube (remember NBC insisting that YouTube remove the Saturday Night Live music video for "Lazy Sunday"?) or peer-to-peer file-sharing networks. While many smaller content creators decided to put their work on YouTube or iTunes, the big media companies dragged their feet – and likely lost billions to piracy, instead of making billions from ad revenue and digital purchases. They've started playing catch-up with sites like Hulu (launched by Fox and NBC in 2008), but there are still hundreds of movies and TV shows that aren't available, legally at least, in digital form.

Sometimes, the behavioral shift involves the ascendance of a new marketplace like eBay or Etsy. When buyers suddenly get comfortable making purchases on a new site like these, often, the artists and craftspeople who are first to set up shop gain an edge. They start accumulating positive feedback and ratings, and they learn about what sells and what doesn't. That trustworthy reputation makes it more likely that people will buy from them, and that knowledge of what buyers want lets them spend their time more efficiently.

Pay attention to these behavioral shifts in how people communicate and consume. There's always a way for you to take advantage of them to build your audience, make new kinds of things, or earn more money.

> What's Free and What Costs?

A big question among artists is how much they should give away for free on their Web site, and what they should charge for.

Obviously, samples are important in persuading someone to purchase an album or a movie. And clearly, the old approach is no longer relevant, where the only taste you got before laying your money down was the lead single on the radio or a trailer on TV.

Some people argue that you can essentially give away a complete work for free online, and still have fans purchase it, either just because they want to support you or because they want it in a more convenient format (a DVD as opposed to a YouTube stream, for instance).

You could imagine seeing a huge promotional boost by giving a different MP3 exclusively to a different influential music blog over the course of a few weeks, until every song on your new album was available online for free.

But some people believe in whetting the audience's appetite with smaller tastes, like the first ten pages of a novel, or a flawless video performance of a magic trick – without the explanation of how its done. I fall more into that camp; I've never given away my books for free in digital form, but I do post excerpts and bonus material starting with the publication date and adding more for a few months afterward.

Jonathan Coulton gave away the MP3s of songs that were part his year-long "Thing a Week" series, but later packaged them up into albums that could be purchased as paid downloads – and also individual CDs and a $50 box set that included all 52 songs. Other bands are content with streaming versions of their songs on their MySpace page, or the 30-second preview available on iTunes.

Filmmaker Tiffany Shlain found that sales of her short film "The Tribe" on DVD actually dropped when a free streaming version was taken off the Sundance Film Festival's Web site.

There's no perfect answer when it comes to determining how much you should give away to spark the most possible interest in (and sales of) a new piece of work. You need to experiment to see what works for you and your audience.

> "When it comes to circulating complimentary copies to bloggers, journalists, and other taste-makers, don't be stingy."

When it comes to circulating complimentary copies to bloggers, journalists, and other taste-makers who may help promote your stuff, though, don't be stingy. You'll usually find that mailing a CD, DVD, or book, or creating a password-protected digital version, for these influencers will pay off many times over.

> Offer Various Versions, and Various Levels of Investment

The 2007 documentary *Helvetica* told the story of one of the world's most widely-used typefaces. On the film's Web site, there are about a dozen different items to purchase, from the regular old DVD ($20) to the Blu-ray DVD ($26) to a limited-edition, specially-designed, autographed Blu-ray DVD ($125.) There is a $20 poster of the film, and several $125 limited-edition prints (most of which have sold out.) There is a t-shirt and a tote bag (both $20.) You can also rent or buy the movie on iTunes.

For his 2009 film, *Objectified*, about the way products are designed, *Helvetica* director Gary Hustwit offers a similar smorgasbord of items. But while the film was in production, he also dangled the opportunity to join a "special group of friends": for $500, you could attend a sneak preview screening of the film, received several limited-edition products related to the film, and get a "thank you" in the film's credits.

Selling just one thing is old hat. Sure, some fans will just want the "mainstay" product – the DVD, coffee-table book, or album you've made. But others will be interested in buying ancillary products (and some super-fans will want to own everything you produce.)

Compiling a book of your photographs? Perhaps a filmmaker friend will produce an hour-long video showing you at work on location, and an interview where you talk about your process and tell some stories. You might release a tour diary alongside a live concert album. Soundtrack CDs can accompany DVD releases...or novels, if you have a talented friend who wants to write a score for your book.

Sometimes, these ancillary products may be designed for educational use. When Tiffany Shlain released her short film "The Tribe" on DVD, she offered a standard DVD version for $25. (The 18-minute film, screened at Sundance, deals with contemporary Jewish identity.) A $299 version for classroom use includes a 50-page teaching guide and a set of "conversation cards" intended to stimulate discussion.

In that vein, you might decide to bundle up 10 or 20 of your books, along with a discussion guide, for book groups.

Thinking about how different non-profit and activist groups frequently have monthly meetings, filmmakers Robert Bahar and Almudena Carracedo created a special package when they released their 2008 documentary *Made in L.A.* (The documentary is about a campaign to improve working conditions in Los Angeles sweatshops where clothing is made.) For $198, a group can get movie posters, postcards, and 21 DVDs. The posters and postcards are intended to be use to promote a screening of the film. By selling twenty of the DVDs for $20 each at the screening, a group can not only cover the cost of the kit, but raise as much as $200 for its own purposes.

When singer-songwriter Jill Sobule was raising money online for her 2009 release, *California Years*, she created various levels at which a supporter could contribute. For $10, you received a free digital download of the album when it was released. For $200, you got free admission to all Sobule's 2008 shows, a t-shirt identifying you as a junior executive producer, and an advance copy of the CD. The levels ascended to the $10,000 "Weapons-Grade Plutonium Level," which included an opportunity to come and sing on the CD, after some coaching from Sobule. And yes, one of Sobule's fans did contribute at that level, although the most popular donation level was $50.

Now, you probably don't want to dedicate your life to developing seventeen different cuts of your movie to sell to fans ("director's cut," "producer's cut," "gaffer's cut," etc.), or endless CDs full of chestnuts from the vaults. But it is worth thinking about whether there are things you could sell that your fans might appreciate.

> "The $10,000 'Weapons-Grade Plutonium Level' included an opportunity to come and sing on the CD..."

Different items, and different levels of support, can do two things: satisfy your fans and make them feel like they're supporting your work, and increase the average amount they spend when they visit your site – which enables you to keep on trucking.

> Do-It-Yourself, or Get Some Help?

Based on how deep you want to dig into the world of self-publishing and distribution, there are roughly three choices you can make. (See the section called "Exploring the New Business Models" for more detail.)

The easiest approach, and also the one that offers you the smallest slice of revenue, is to use a service that will manufacture and ship your work on demand. All you need to do is upload your finished book, CD, t-shirt design, or DVD. Two good examples of this kind of service are CreateSpace, owned by Amazon, and CafePress. The benefit is that you're free to focus on things other than manufacturing and shipping – like trying to sell the heck out of your latest release. Companies like Amazon also already have many buyers' credit card info on file, which removes one small obstacle to a purchase.

The second-easiest approach is to supervise the production of your products, using a local printer or a CD/DVD replication firm. This tends to give you a cheaper per-unit price than the first option, which means you get more profit. You also have more choices about how your product is made – a thicker cotton sweatshirt, for instance, or a leather-textured cover for your hardcover book. Once you've made a batch of product, you hand it over to a fulfillment house, which receives incoming orders from fans and ships the products out. The only issue here is estimating how many copies of a given item you'll sell; you could be left with unsold inventory that you'll have to discount or ditch.

The third approach, which will get the most dirt under your fingernails (but also can supply you with the best returns), is supervising the manufacturing yourself, and handling the fulfillment on your own (or with help from a part time employee, family member, or intern.) You'll be responsible for finding the shopping cart software you want to incorporate into your site, making sure that orders go out in a timely way, and dealing with returns and other customer service issues. But you'll keep the most possible profit on every item you sell – and you'll have the opportunity to sign items or include a personal "thanks for your support" note with each order, which can really build loyalty.

(With the second and third approaches – doing most of it yourself and doing all of it yourself – you might also choose a little-known way to get your books, CDs, or DVDs sold on Amazon. You can sign up to be a seller on Amazon, and pay a Amazon a slice of every sale plus a monthly fee, without using Amazon-owned CreateSpace to manufacture the items. This lets you control quality, and in most cases will give you more profit. See http://www.amazonservices.com/content/sell-on-amazon.htm.)

When selling digital downloads, which obviously don't require manufacturing, you can choose to use a company like CreateSpace or CD Baby, which will handle everything for you and get your work into digital marketplaces like iTunes and Amazon. However, to get the most revenue from selling downloads, you should use a service like E-Junkie or PayLoadz, which handle payment and file storage, but depend on you to generate traffic – since you don't benefit from the shopping and searching activity on a site like iTunes or Amazon.

None of these approaches will guarantee success, or doom you to failure. You may find that you can drive very high volumes of purchases, and that having someone else handle all the manufacturing and shipping keeps you saner. Or you may find that with a smaller fan base, it makes more sense for you to create a limited-edition run of 1000 CDs for every release, and use a fulfillment house to get orders to people.

And you may find, as novelists Lisa Genova and Brunonia Barry have, that using self-publishing and self-distribution as a stepping stone to a publishing contract (or record contract, or movie contract) eliminates all your headaches, gives you a hefty advance, and lets you live the creative life you want, writing in your office and venturing out on the occasional promotional tour that you don't have to arrange.

Trying different things, and seeing how they affect your creative output and your monthly income, will lead you to the right answer for you.

> Embrace Conversations, Instead of Delivering a Monologue

All these new platforms and conduits aren't just about one-way communication, allowing you to send out Facebook status updates about bookstore signings, Twitter messages about live TV appearances, and e-mail newsletters about your acceptance into a prestigious film festival.

Your fans will have questions. They'll want to congratulate you, or offer an assist, or suggest an idea for your next book that you may or may not use.

> "Accessibility is a huge difference between the artists of the 20th century and the artists of the 21st century."

So it's important to be accessible. Accessibility is a huge difference between the artists of the 20th century, where the best you could hope for as a fan was a form letter and a machine-signed 8-by-10 glossy, and the artists of the 21st century. It makes people feel that they're part of your team, as opposed to just purchasing your product.

For some artists, accessibility means responding to every e-mail – even if the response is a quick "thanks for your message," or a link to an answer that you've given a zillion times before on your Frequently Asked Questions page.

For others, when the flood of e-mail gets too intense to reply to every one, they might choose instead to respond to a comment here and there on their blog, or participate regularly in the discussion forums on their site. Cartoonist Dylan Meconis produces an occasional podcast where she addresses readers' questions, for example.

Some artists also opt to set up various e-mail addresses to direct certain kinds of messages to specific folders in their inbox. Messages to pr@yoursite.com ought to produce a quick response, since they likely come from folks who want to give you press. Notes to plotideas@yoursite.com might go into a special folder that you look at when you're in need of inspiration.

It's important to keep in mind that your relationship with your audience is a conversation, not a monologue. That conversation engenders loyalty. And when you become too distant or infrequent a conversationalist, fans start drifting away.

> Take the Cannoli

Once you've begun to cultivate your online community, and your career is starting to grow, you may find you get offers from the old power players: publishers, art dealers, movie distributors.

The money can be alluring. These guys still have deep pockets, and they can offer attractive advance payments, and the possibility of having your work seen by a mass audience.

There's nothing wrong with exploring these opportunities. Often, they can provide the financial support that you need to keep working on your art full-time, or to fund the big project you've always wanted to take on. For Lisa Genova, who self-published her first novel, *Still Alice*, the goal all along was to get an established publisher to pick it up and reprint it, so she could reach a wider audience (and, of course, make more money.) Multimedia artist Ze Frank signed a movie deal with Universal to get the chance to write his very own feature film for a studio. YouTube personality Michael Buckley inked a contract with HBO Labs to break out of his little YouTube window, and develop new kinds of material.

But it's important to understand the details: who will own the work you're going to create? (Or, more specifically, who will own which rights?) How much will you make from every sale? Will you be allowed to purchase books or CDs or DVDs at a discounted rate, and sell them through your own site? How will your new partner promote your work, and how will you work to support them? How long are you committed to working with them? (I.E., if things don't go well, do you have an "out"?)

Perhaps the most important thing is not handing over the relationship with your audience. Ideally, even if your new partner wants to build a flashy new Web site for you, you will still keep blogging at the same address you always have (even if there's a copy of your blog that becomes part of the new site), or Twittering as before. You want to avoid having your identity disappear from one place and then reappear somewhere else; that can seem as though you've been co-opted by The Man.

Control of your mailing list or audience database is also crucial. Obviously, you may want to promote the work you do with your new partner to your existing fan base. But you most likely won't want the PR folks at the record label or movie studio to start blasting out thrice-weekly e-mails to your fans, who will quickly start unsubscribing. If your new partner wants to start building an e-mail list of its own, can you get access to those names – or are they purely the partner's property?

Avoiding audience backlash is a delicate job once you've signed on to work with a big-time publisher, movie studio, or record label. How can you ensure that your audience doesn't feel you've sold out, or abandoned them? One key is to keep communicating with them as frequently as you have in the past, and through the same channels – and avoid letting tone-deaf "professional" marketers and PR people start pitching the audience on your behalf.

"Taking the cannoli" is my term (borrowed, of course, from *The Godfather*) for figuring out how a partnership with an established marketing or distribution entity can build your career, raise your profile, and provide you with income – without sacrificing the strong relationship you've forged with your audience, or giving up your creative objectives.

> Experiment (Cheaply) to Figure Out What Works

Successful artists online are constantly experimenting in many different ways, and tuning in to feedback about what is resonating with their audiences.

They experiment artistically, trying new genres, styles, participatory strategies, and formats - and paying attention to whether people seem to dig what they're doing. Artist Natasha Wescoat was initially painting large, abstract works - until she tried doing contemporary landscapes in a more fun and whimsical style, which became her trademark.

They also experiment with business models and revenue streams. Do DVDs sell well, but people complain when you put short ads in front of your videos? Do certain kinds of

> "Business models that work for a time can also stop working."

merchandise sell better than others? Will people happily pay an extra $5 for autographed CDs? You may find that fulfilling products yourself doesn't work well, and that it makes more sense to hire a fulfillment house. Just about anything is worth a try, as long as you pay attention to whether it's worth the time and trouble, and how your fans are responding.

And business models that work for a time can also stop working. When JibJab Media's business of licensing content to other Web sites started to dry up, and advertising didn't seem like it was going to generate enough revenue to support the kind of work they wanted to do, they developed a subscription-based e-card product line.

Artists also experiment with different ways to connect with their audiences. What platforms are most effective, what's the right frequency, and what other sites attract people likely to appreciate your work? Novelist Sarah Mlynowski says she has "joined a hundred different social networks, trying to see what works. If there's a pull on the line, I stick with it."

Production, promotion, distribution - there are lots of other dimensions for experimentation. Just do it cheaply (at the start), and pay attention to whether it seems to be striking a chord with your audience - and then invest more of your time and energy in doing more of it.

> ## > Be Patient: Building an Audience Takes Time

If you're reading this book, you are likely not in a position to spend $10 million buying national TV and print ads to promote yourself, or hiring blimps to alert Super Bowl attendees about your latest release.

Building an audience using these free and inexpensive strategies takes time. People are out there who will appreciate what you're doing; it just may take them time for you to discover one another. If you're making remarkable stuff, a small audience will inevitably grow.

Having a huge viral hit that gets passed around the planet, of course, is a nice way to increase your audience size overnight. But those are very hard to engineer. And even people who've been lucky to have their work "go viral," as happened in 2004 with JibJab's "This Land" video, have often been cranking out work and cultivating an audience for years (JibJab was founded in 1999.) Without the list of 130,000 e-mail addresses they'd built up over those five years, it's a good bet that "This Land" wouldn't have reached escape velocity.

Jill Sobule and Robert Greenwald, two artists who've been able to raise substantial sums of money from their audiences to fund new projects, have both been working in their fields – and expanding their fan bases – for years. Sobule's first album came out in 1990, and Greenwald began directing made-for-TV movies in 1977. Dave Kellet, who draws the online comic "Sheldon," started it in the late 1990s; it wasn't until 2006 that he felt comfortable enough with the revenue it was generating to quit his highly-paid day job as a toy designer.

If traffic to your site isn't doubling every month, or you are still getting an average of 0.4 comments on your blog every week, don't give up hope. Try something new. Tweak your style. Be outrageous. Come up with a new way of engaging with the audience you do have. Reach out to other sites where your kind of people hang out and establish new partnerships.

Building a big audience isn't like mixing a mug of instant coffee. It's like vigilantly-tended, painstakingly-sorted, lovingly-roasted, perfectly-ground coffee beans, knowledgably brewed into a great cuppa java.

It takes effort, but the results are worth it. Before long, you'll be among the small cluster of artists who have forged a new kind of bond with their fan base, and who understand what it takes to cultivate a successful creative career in this noisy new era.

Table: Defining the Terms

The two big challenges this book aims to address are: how do you build a fan base online, and how can that fan base support your career? Here are some of the terms I use in thinking about those challenges.

The artist	That's you.
The work	What you choose to make.
The audience	The people who support your career – and may participate in your creative process in some way. You may prefer to think of them as your "community," your "collaborators," your supporters, your benefactors, etc. A big part of your audience will be passive, but some will want to be more engaged or active.
The platform(s)	Where can people find you online? Where do you connect and communicate with your audience? One platform might be your own Web site; another might be YouTube or a blog.
The conduit(s)	A conduit is a direct connection to your audience – like an e-mail list or RSS feed – that allows you to communicate with them when you'd like, rather than waiting for them to return to your Web site.
The partners	People or groups that help you expand your audience. A partner could be a blog that writes a review of your latest project, or a non-profit group that offers to promote you to their mailing list.
The distribution channels and marketplaces	These are the places where your work is sold. You might choose only to sell through your own site, or you might use various distribution channels and marketplaces like iTunes, Amazon, Etsy, etc.
The business model	The mix of revenue streams that support your career: speaking fees, CD/DVD sales, merchandise, etc.

Introduction to the Interviews

I've excerpted here thirty of the most interesting (and hopefully, helpful) interviews I conducted while researching this book. All of them took place in 2008 and 2009.

I think that whatever field you're in, you will be able to glean some ideas and inspiration from most of the people here. A novelist may have tried something that'll be useful to you as a musician. A cartoonist may be able to learn something from what *didn't* work for a filmmaker. I'd strongly suggest that you check out each artist's Web site to get a taste for their work, and see exactly how they're building an audience around it and generating revenue.

How did I decide whom to interview? Of course, I asked the readers of my blog CinemaTech to make suggestions. But I also tried to identify people who have built up a substantial audience online, are collaborating with that audience in new ways, and are making some decent money – even if a few of them still haven't yet quit their day jobs.

I steered clear of including too many artists who are doing cool stuff in the digital realm, but who relied on traditional media players (like publishers, record labels, and movie studios) to build up their fan base in the first place. I wanted to focus more on people who've developed innovative and effective strategies that can work without an assist from The Man.

Michael Buckley
Creator of "What the Buck"

When I spoke with Michael Buckley in May 2008, he'd already figured out how to build a big audience on YouTube and earn more money from the site's "Partner Program" (which shares ad revenue with content creators) than he was earning at his day job. On his three-

times-a-week "What the Buck" show, Buckley became the Internet's cattiest, cleverest pop culture commentator, with more than 300,000 people subscribing to his YouTube channel.

Buckley told me he liked the balance of working a regular desk job during the day and producing his show in his spare time. But he also alluded to a development deal that was in the works. By September 2008, HBO Labs announced that it had signed up Buckley to come up with new concepts for TV and the Web. In December, he inked a deal with Sony Pictures Television to produce a monthly online show, "Minisode Maniac," for the Minisode Network, which presents condensed versions of classic TV shows.

Though he kept on producing videos for his YouTube audience, he decided to quit his day job.

★ ★ ★ ★ ★

I was doing a weekly cable access television show, "Table for Two," in the summer of 2006, with a female co-host. I had ambitions of something happening. I knew that I probably wouldn't get cast in things as an unknown, and that I needed some sort of demo footage. It was a one-hour live show, and in every episode, I did a five-minute celebrity rant called "What the Buck."

I didn't know what YouTube was. But my cousin posted one of the "What the Buck" videos there. I didn't even think about it. It was embedded on my MySpace page, and people started leaving comments, like "you should do this more." I felt encouraged. My cousin was posting the segments once a week. Then I started doing them four or five times a week, and I started posting them on YouTube myself.

Building an audience. I'd get eight comments on a video, and I'd be thrilled. The first time I had a video with 1000 views, I was out of my mind. I always enjoyed the progress of getting more views, and more subscribers. When I got 100,000 views for a video, I really thought, "That's it."

With "Table for Two," who knew how many were watching in the part of Connecticut where you could see it? People in the grocery store said they enjoyed it.

Then, in spring of 2007, when I started covering "American Idol," my videos started getting a lot of press, and YouTube notice. At that point, I knew that "What the Buck" was something separate and large. I got on the front page of the Hartford *Courant.*

I still had my day job, the same admin job I'd had for the last six years, a 10-to-6 office job. They were very flexible, but they didn't know the extent to which I was working on the YouTube stuff.

One thing that seemed to work was saying shocking things. On YouTube, people don't want to just hear the news, like "Entertainment Tonight." You have to have some sort of edge, or an ability to make it humorous. I couldn't just say, "Britney Spears got arrested today." It was more about me making it silly.

My first video that really took off was "Beyoncé Threatens to Kill Jennifer Hudson for Winning Oscar." People were searching on the movie *Dreamgirls* because it had been leaked to YouTube, and they found me. I got so many e-mails – lots of them hate mail – and I know Jennifer Hudson saw it.

Promotion. Back in the early days, I was definitely actively promoting the videos – posting comments on other people's videos and MySpace pages, saying, "Hey, check out my videos." For months I was actively doing that, and I had five seconds of opening credits to my videos, where I said, "Rate it even if you hate it," and "Please subscribe." In the video, I might say, "Hey guys, do me a favor – give this video five stars and leave a comment."

My videos started showing up on YouTube's top-rated page, even before I had 10,000 subscribers to my YouTube Channel.

You might say, "Oh, you're begging." I don't care. Most people who were watching didn't know they were supposed to rate it or leave a comment. Now, everybody does that – they say, please rate my video and subscribe to my channel.

Traditional media exposure. Even when I've been in national magazines or newspapers, or had stories about me on the CW or Fox, I get one or two e-mails. Any traditional press I've ever gotten doesn't really affect my YouTube audience. It's totally Internet-based. You can be in traditional media, and it's not getting people to go to your YouTube page. And when you go on TV, it's just not as much fun. On the Internet, you have real interaction with people.

> "Any traditional press I've ever gotten doesn't really affect my YouTube audience. It's totally Internet-based."

I started doing some live broadcasting, too, on Blog.tv, twice a week, at 10 PM Eastern. That started in 2008. I broadcast from my webcam, and people ask me questions. I sing, I dance, I do crazy stuff. The first hour is more planned out. I'll play music, and give advice. The last half hour is for people who just want to stay. There are typically about 5,000 people watching, but only 150 people can get in the chat room to interact with me.

I also started a personal vlog channel on YouTube, under the user name peron75. That was my original YouTube account. People can see me as myself. I'm more laid back, not that judgmental or bitchy. Hopefully, people think, "Oh, this guy is O.K." I talk about my life, and the show. I ask viewers questions, and address their video responses, and ask them to respond to me.

Doing the correct things. If I were to pick my key moments on doing the correct things, in terms of getting lots of subscribers, one is that I'm present in the YouTube community. You can't just throw a video up there and hope that people will watch it. When people leave me comments, I reply to them, and they see that I'm there.

I post three videos a week. You have to continue with your content.

Now, I get over 100 e-mails a day. There's no way I can reply to all of them. I try to write back, or address things on the live show. You can't just be some TV show, some guy with a green screen in his house.

Good money. I do make good money on YouTube, from the YouTube partners program. [By the end of 2008, Buckley was earning more than $100,000 from the site, according to the New York *Times*.] I generally make more on YouTube than I do at my day job. But at my job, I have five weeks paid vacation, and YouTube doesn't offer that. I'm socking the money into a 401k – I'm no fool. I think part of the appeal is, he has got a real job. I like the security, and it keeps it all balanced.

I love doing this. I love Internet video. As long as my audience continues, I see doing this as long as I possibly can. When I take the weekend off, I miss it.

I would never have gotten that kind of satisfaction if I were just the host of some TV show. There's something about reaching this global audience. If I had a TV show on cable, at 10 PM on the Oxygen channel, no one's going to watch it. But I'm on the Internet every single day, and there's something cool about that.

Mike Chapman
Animator and Writer, "Homestar Runner"

The Brothers Chaps, as Mike and Matt Chapman are known, are the creative forces behind the wildly-successful Web property Homestar Runner, which features a new cartoon every week, online games, and a merchandise shop that supports the venture. (The Brothers Chaps are very much anti-advertising.) Their characters, especially Strong Bad, The Cheat, and Homestar, have become Web celebs. They've collaborated with the band They Might Be Giants and recently released their first videogame with Telltale Games. The Brothers Chaps are based in Atlanta. I spoke with Mike (he's on the left in the photo), the older of the two.

★ ★ ★ ★ ★

We have very much been of the mindset that if you concentrate on the product, and if the product is good, things will happen.

For the first several years of "Homestar Runner," we had other jobs. That gave it time to grow naturally, by word-of-mouth.

Origins. The characters and the whole world were created in 1996 by me and Craig Zobel. We were working at the Atlanta Olympics, for the Australian Sports Network, and we were bored. Together, we made a children's book. Everything in it was done with a Sharpie marker. We didn't have a scanner, and I didn't have a computer of my own, so we really just cut-and-pasted it all together. We made ten or twelve black-and-white copies at Kinko's, with a color cover, and we gave them to friends.

In late 1999, Matt and I were learning Flash and Illustrator, wanting to become graphic designers. We used "Homestar" as the subject matter while we were learning Flash. At the time, I was trying to freelance, doing litigation graphics for courtrooms. I worked on a lot of mesothelioma cases. I drew a lot of lungs.

In January of 2000, HomestarRunner.com went live. We had maybe two or three games there, and some short cartoons. It was on my personal MindSpring page for a while, and then we actually bought the domain. We put it up, and e-mailed our friends.

Then, Shockwave chose it as their Site of the Day, which was huge. It spiked our traffic. But a week later, we were back down to nine people visiting. We got mentioned in some British Internet magazine. I remember when somebody we didn't know would e-mail us about the site. That was awesome. Or we'd find people who had linked to our site, and we didn't even know them. It was kind of a steady, natural growth.

Avoiding advertising. We had nothing for sale, though – no way to make money. Even at that point, we didn't like ads. Pretty early on, there were Flash cartoons that would force you to watch an ad before the cartoon, or they'd say "Sponsored by this company." If there was a way to keep going without resorting to that, we were all for it.

> "When we first did t-shirts, people would send us a check, and our dad would go to the post office and put five or ten shirts into the mail at a time."

We did the cartoons for two years before we started making any shirts. We just loved doing it. There were lots of times where I'd rather sit home and make cartoons than do anything else. Flash and the Internet were so exciting to us. We definitely liked hearing from people in e-mails. But even if we hadn't gotten feedback, I think we would've kept doing what we were doing.

When we first did t-shirts, people would send us a check, and our dad would go to the post office and put five or ten shirts into the mail at a time. Over 2001 and 2002, those numbers started to grow. Then, Matt quit his day job in mid-2002. I was still doing freelance, but I'd only take a freelance client if it was really fun. We did a music video for They Might Be Giants, after they contacted us and said they were fans. We've continued to work with them.

With the music videos we've animated, we got paid for most of them. Not to the point where it was making us tons of money, but it was also something we wanted to do.

In early 2002, we started doing a cartoon every Monday – a weekly update. Before that, it was more random. A few weeks or a month or two might go by in between updates.

Most of our income has been from t-shirts and DVDs, and whatever other merchandise we sell in the store. Our multi-DVD sets do well, as does the Trogdor shirt. Starting in 2003, we got a fulfillment company [Fulfillment Strategies International] to handle all the orders, rather than doing it out of our parents' basement. Our sister deals with the fulfillment house and the t-shirt printers. Matt and I, the less we see of that, the better.

We put a button on our site to let people know when we have a new product. We just try to sell stuff that we would want to buy if we were fans – not a pillow or a sleeping bag just because we can. I think most people understand that that's how we make our living.

But we don't advertise the store at the end of our videos or anything. We could've made more money if we pushed the store more, but I wouldn't have felt good about it.

DVD releases. Our first DVD came out in Christmas of 2004. We hired a friend of ours who had done DVD authoring, and conversion of stuff from Flash files to uncompressed AVIs. We taught ourselves about how to make the Flash stuff look good on TV.

That was after we'd done a hundred of the Strong Bad E-mails. [Strong Bad is a gruff and sardonic character who answers readers' inquiries.] Now, every 30 or 40 e-mails, we put out another one.

I've never really been on Facebook or MySpace, though there are some fan-created pages on MySpace. We've put up a few things on YouTube. We're doing a videogame for the [Nintendo] Wii, and we did a teaser cartoon for that and put it on YouTube. That went up a week or two before we announced the game, "Strong Bad's Cool Game for Attractive People."

Here's how the game happened. Telltale Games in San Francisco contacted us. We were fans of their "Sam & Max" games. We wanted to make sure there was a good fit. It's a five-episode project, and we were very involved, which is cool. They listen to us when we have ideas – it's not just like they licensed the characters. There's talking, so Matt has done a lot of the audio.

> "We always make the cartoons on Sundays and put them up right when they're done. There's an immediacy to it."

I don't look at discussion forums and comments about the show, because one negative comment can negate fifty good comments. You run into people who say that we jumped the shark five years ago.

Moving fast. We always make the cartoons on Sundays and put them up right when they're done. There's an immediacy to it. Normally, something you watch on TV has been finished weeks and months before you ever see it. We write and record everything within the day before you're watching it. It gives a freshness to the content. It hasn't been over-written and over-thought by twenty different people.

How do we evaluate proposals about new projects, or collaborations? We learned how to politely say no to things that were going to affect our lives negatively. If it's going to be fun, if we're going to enjoy doing it, and if the end project is going to be something we want to have happen, we say "yes."

Ze Frank
Multimedia Artist and Creator of "theshow"

With silent-film-era wide eyes, an *Alice in Wonderland* sense of whimsy, and an Internet-era dose of irony, Ze Frank is a writer and artist who has chosen the Web his medium. His animations, collaborative art projects, and videos have been seen by millions, and he has spoken at events like the annual TED Conference and South by Southwest. His daily videoblog, "theshow with zefrank," ran for exactly a year, from 2006 to 2007, and featured challenges and projects that invited viewers to get involved. The success of "theshow" led to representation from the United Talent Agency, which has enabled him to chase opportunities in the entertainment industry.

★ ★ ★ ★ ★

I was working in New York for Dennis Interactive, which was a full-service interactive agency. I had an arts background, and the Web was just super-exciting. I was working with animators, and I had a little programming knowledge from college. I started to play around, creating these interactive toys. Then, as an invitation to my birthday party, I created this animated graphic called "How to Dance Properly." That was in 2001. It went totally ape shit after I sent it to a few friends. It got e-mailed everywhere. It was hosted on an Earthlink free account, which went down within twelve hours. There was no zefrank.com at the time.

Taking the leap. I'd been itching to move out of Dennis. I felt like I could go freelance, and I left in 2001.

In the freelance world, I had so much time to myself, mainly because I didn't have a huge client roster. I started spending all my time being fascinated with the audience that was coming to my site, and trying to figure out if I could keep that audience, and what the dynamics of popularity online were. I really had no clue what was going on. This notion of being "viral" wasn't really in the vernacular.

The question was, "How do you connect with people?"

The first thing that I stupidly though was, "You just release a lot of stuff." I spent eight or nine months where I stopped freelancing and just made shit. I tried to do a project every day, and have a new thing on the site.

I was doing some projects based on e-mails. Someone would say, "Make me a dragon," and I'd do it and post it. But that's not really scalable. I was chasing the big numbers, trying to get large audiences to come back.

I started a mailing list, and had a very prominent "e-mail me" link on the site.

I'd take the odd job making ad banners, to pay the bills. I did some low-level consulting and project work, and I got larger and larger projects. I did sites for Russell Wong, and worked for Dakota Jackson, creating interactive software for his SoHo gallery.

Exploring participation. Eventually, I started to focus on the Web as a participation platform, creating these participatory projects. I did "When Office Supplies Attack," which was a contest where people sent me pictures of themselves being attacked by office supplies. We did a toilet paper fashion show. There was "The Letter Project," where people took a picture with themselves holding the first letter of their last name, and with those letters we created a ransom note-generator. I did a collage-maker, where you could collage people's faces together.

> "Eventually, I started to focus on the Web as a participation platform."

I put message boards on the site, which gave me a real, live experience of community. Ostensibly, the boards were focused on the site, but my activities weren't really coherent enough to foster long-term conversation. It was basically a community of people talking amongst themselves.

Then, I started experimenting with different ways to communicate with people through the message boards. We had "The Fiction Project," which was collaborative fiction. People on the boards could create their own rule sets for writing fiction, like one person would write two words, and then another person would write two words.

I definitely cared about the traffic to the site. For a time there, from 2002 to 2004, I would use a mailing list whenever I released a new project I was psyched about. I could definitely see a bounce in traffic when I e-mailed people. At the time, it was thousands of people. Now, it's in the tens of thousands. But I haven't sent an update in a couple years.

The mailing list represented a portion of the population that wanted to be reminded of something after they walk away.

I really don't know why I was doing all this stuff, other than because it was exciting, and I knew that the alternative was working in an office, which wasn't that attractive.

I didn't see any straightforward way to make money.

Speaking gigs. But a couple things I did got press, and then I started getting asked to do speaking gigs, because I was doing stuff that interested people in the arts world and the advertising world. So I started talking about it.

After a couple gigs, I realized that it would be a lot more fun to do speaking gigs in a humorous way. So I started creating a brand and a persona, using some of the tonality of the site. Then, I picked up a speaking agent, The Leigh Bureau.

I was watching online video progress, and I was really interested in the role that audience could play in shaping a show. But there wasn't much coming out that really involved the audience in a significant way.

I was speaking at a conference in Lisbon for FremantleMedia [which produces TV shows like "American Idol."] I started wondering, could you make something that didn't have a format at all – just let the format evolve over time? I figured I'd try something really short. The average viewing time, I was told, was seven seconds. I had no idea what I was going to do. I just turned on the camera, and I would talk about the news. I didn't try to write it or plan it. But I did try to be reactive to the audience. That's how it grew. Eventually, you wind up with a format whether you like it or not.

I created this device called "Something from the Comments," where I would react to people who left comments. I wanted to inhabit the world together with the audience, and I'd use the comments as a starting point.

I played a game of chess against my audience. We did "Earth Sandwich," where I challenged the audience to put two pieces of bread directly opposite from each other on the planet. You could go look at the latitude and longitude of any place on earth and find out what place was exactly opposite. So people sent in pictures. Within two weeks, a team in New Zealand and Spain did it, and sent documentation. We had "The Running Fool Project," where a guy went across the country and back using viewers of the show for lodging. Most of that was facilitated by the audience.

In a way, the show was a veneer, a central rallying point, for this community. I only produced three minutes of media per day.

Business models. It didn't have a business model in the first five months. I was trying to wrap my head around that. You had Revver just coming out [which offered to share ad revenue with creators]. I switched over to hosting my videos on Revver, and started making some money from their ads. But then, I started being much more aggressive about it. In the actual videos, I'd say, "Hey, anybody want to sponsor me?" And I started looking for sponsors. I did a few sponsorships with GoDaddy.com, and Dewars came in and sponsored the archives.

> "'theshow' didn't have a business model in the first five months. I was trying to wrap my head around that."

I also created "Gimme Some Candy," which was a kind of micro-sponsorship. People could buy these little images of ducks in $5, $10, $25, and $50 increments. Each duck would include 110 characters they could play with, so they could write a little thing that would show up on the site. I was also selling text ads on the site through AdBrite.

The Revver revenue fell off at a certain point, so I went over to Blip.tv. They facilitate serving the videos, and they provide an ad network service.

I absolutely felt like I was making a living. I only really capitalized on "theshow" for seven months. But it was the most money I'd ever made.

Within the first week of "theshow," I said it'd only be a year long. It felt to me like nothing ever ends on the Internet. I thought it'd be cool to think of a project in a time-limited way. By the time six months rolled around, I was of two minds. It had really sunk in how hard this was, and at the same time, I was getting all this press, and it was going so well. It was making money. I thought, "Maybe I should continue."

But I felt like to make it sustainable, physically and spiritually, I'd have had to bring on other people, and change the format, not have so many inside jokes. And it wouldn't have been "theshow" anymore.

Agent shopping. Before "theshow" started, I'd been approached by National Geographic to host something, and so we pitched a show together. I'd also auditioned for some other stuff, and I had a manager in LA. He said, "You should really have an agent." So we went shopping for agents. It was the most freaky, disappointing experience.

The stereotype was really true. It was like the guy from *Jerry McGuire*. These guys threw lots of information at you, and most of them had no idea about the Internet. One group was a bunch of older agents who wanted to get into the game. They said, "You teach us." It felt a little fake and weird.

United Talent Agency called me out of the blue. They flew out to New York. I really liked them, so that's who I signed with.

We met with people like [former ABC and Yahoo executive] Lloyd Braun, [ex-Disney CEO] Michael Eisner, and [DreamWorks Animation head] Jeffrey Katzenberg, talking about making videos for the Internet. But the way of structuring a new kind of business, and thinking about advertising, got very complicated. It wasn't clear to me how to make these properties viable.

I signed a deal to write a feature [film] for a production company that is based at Universal. I wrote a movie over the last year, interrupted by the Writer's Guild strike. Then, my contact at Universal left to go to MGM, and the project got orphaned. Then, my agent left United Talent Agency to go to Endeavor. So now I'm technically with Endeavor.

A lot of the excitement and thrill I had has been replaced with a more sober realization that this is a hard business.

Two approaches to growth. There are two different ways to think about growth. One is the long shot model: "I'm going to bang my head against the wall until I hit a jackpot." That's the classic model for the artist, regardless of the industry, and not many people hit that jackpot.

The other model for growth is, I'm going to create something myself and do it on my own terms, and build an audience and try to get reliable [financial] returns from it.

> "There's this conversational aspect of the relationship between the creator and the audience, and between one audience member and another."

The long shot is very attractive, and not only for monetary reasons. It pulls you forward in a way. It keeps your spirit alive in the dreamworld. It helps me fantasize. So much of entertainment has to do with the notion of possibility, and opportunity. If you're a musician, you're imagining playing in a nicer studio and collaborating with really amazing people.

With the self-sustained model, you have limited options. You know what's in your reach, and what's not.

I really want a mixture of both.

I could spend a lot of time right now making videos – one-offs, or narratives – and keep trying to push Hollywood to pay attention to me. But most of my time is spent trying to explore new kinds of models for entertainment that don't really have obvious financial structures surrounding them. But I think they will.

There's this conversational aspect of the relationship between the creator and the audience, and between one audience member and another. Sometimes, it's not about producing new media for their consumption. The media itself may not matter, but the cross chatter does.

Having people suggest ideas to you, and releasing things before they're ready, to get feedback – the audience is reflecting back to you who you are and what you might become.

That fast feedback loop, the connection to the audience – I wish there was a way to take advantage of that, and also have the resources that Hollywood people do.

I wanted to reverse-engineer a sit-com, and get funding for that. I wanted to create the characters, and then have the characters interact with each other one-on-one, in a series of short vignettes. Forget the narrative arc, and just release them week after week to see what the audience responded to – what kind of character dynamics are funny or touching – and build the story out of that. But traditional TV networks consider that uncertain, even though you can do tons of testing with this and just iterate until you get things right.

I'm kind of scared of YouTube. There's this unmoderated comment stream. It just seems to be a really aggressive place, and you don't control your own traffic. But I am interested in things like Facebook, Flickr, Twitter, FriendFeed, and Tumblr.

For me, experimentation is not about the technology. In an ever-changing technological landscape, where today's platforms are not tomorrow's platforms, the key seems to be that any one of these spaces can use a dose of humanity and art and culture. You have to go in and look at building human things in them, not just playing with the technology or commenting on the technology. They do exist as places for personal expression, and the rules aren't always obvious.

Curt Ellis
Documentary Producer and Writer

In *King Corn*, two buddies move to Iowa and lease an acre of farmland to try their hand at growing corn. That leads them to explore the hidden role that corn plays in the American diet, from fattening up cows to sweetening soft drinks. *King Corn* wound up as one of the most talked-about documentaries of 2007. It premiered at the South by Southwest Film Festival in Austin that spring, had a theatrical release in the fall, and in April 2008 it aired on PBS. I spoke with Curt Ellis, one of the film's stars, who also co-wrote and co-produced it, and Caitlin Boyle, a researcher for the project who also handled marketing and outreach. (Ellis is pictured at right, with Ian Cheney, his co-star and co-writer.)

★ ★ ★ ★ ★

Curt Ellis: They always tell you to start thinking about your audience from Day One, before you ever pick up a camera. We weren't. We were busy trying to figure out how to tell a really complicated story in a way that would be relevant and interesting to our audience – whoever they turned out to be.

Along the way, so many people told us they were interested in the film and wanted to see it and spread the word about it that we started to build this database of people. Eventually, it grew into hundreds of allies, some of whom later became important in the distribution of the film. We just used the software FileMaker to build the database. Then, we created a big e-mail list using Constant Contact [an e-mail marketing service.]

While we were making the film, we'd go do an interview, and the person would say, "Have you seen what the local Slow Food chapter is doing?" We realized there is a Slow Food chapter in almost every city in the country, and that their members were naturally interested in our film. So we started connecting with that built-in audience.

Ricardo Salvador, one of the people we interviewed for the film, wound up working as a program officer at the Kellogg Foundation. I sent him the finished film, because he was in it. He said, "This is the kind of thing we really ought to get behind." They connected us with hundreds of organizations that were interested in what we were doing. They also had us screen the film at their annual conference, the Food & Society Conference, and distribute 600 DVDs to the attendees.

We started getting in touch with various blogs while we were in production. Diane Hatz, who runs the Sustainable Table blog, had heard about our film and wanted us to know about some people she thought would be helpful. We kept in touch as the film started its roll-out. She put something out almost every week. That was a huge part of building momentum.

> "For us, it was really important for the film to be a rallying point for a larger movement."

Other members of the sustainable agriculture community read Diane's stuff. If Diane is excited, then Kerry at Sustainable Scoop gets excited. The blogs helped keep this sense of freshness going. It's very easy for a film to become stagnant.

Communicating with the blogs entailed writing the bloggers friendly notes and asking about their babies. We really became friends with these people. We met with them for coffee when we were in town.

[Co-star and co-writer] Ian [Cheney] and I wrote guest posts for a few blogs. We became faces for the film, because we're in it.

For us, it was really important for the film to be a rallying point for a larger movement. There was a farm bill up for debate in the Senate, and there was all this energy behind sustainable food, the anti-obesity movement, and Slow Food. People wanted to help us all the way through, whether they were bloggers or people who came to screenings and bought DVDs, because they felt we were all involved with the same cause.

Our film premiered at South by Southwest Film Festival in 2007. Then, we did two dozen festivals after that, from Chicago to Sydney. We were selling DVDs during the entire festival run. We always carry DVDs with us in person – me, Ian, and [director] Aaron [Woolf].

When we opened up theatrically in New York and a half-dozen other cities, we took the DVDs off the site. Or at least until three-quarters of the way through. Balcony Releasing handled the theatrical release, and we use the service Neoflix to sell DVDs on our Web site.

We were lucky to get about $500,000 in outreach support from the Kellogg Foundation and other funders. That let us hire some publicisits, and pay our outreach coordinator, and it let us build our Web site, which is the central hub that all these other spokes come out of. We'd add a new feature to the Web site every few weeks. We had a contest where people could edit their own video using some short clips and photos related to the film, to make their own statement about agriculture. The winner got $1000. We also had a 20-minute streaming clip of the film that went on AOL's True Stories Web site, to promote our PBS broadcast. That clip and a trailer were seen more than 60,000 times over a two-week period.

People can donate a copy of the DVD to their local library, organize a community screening, or write to their Congressperson about the farm bill. We also created something called the King Corn Challenge, where Ian and I tried to consume no corn-based products for a month.

Our Web site launched about a month before we opened in theaters, and our blog only took off after that. That felt like it was late.

In terms of digital, our sense was that the Internet download world isn't as valuable now as it will be in the future. But we did a deal with Docurama, where they will launch it electronically on sites like iTunes, and they'll sell a new edition of the DVD with some new extras.

We didn't really use MySpace or Facebook. But it helped to have one dedicated outreach person on our team, Caitlyn, who was constantly thinking, "What can we do to set up community screenings, and keep the blog going?" She was responsible for interacting with the food and agriculture community, because the rest of us got distracted by deliverables for getting different versions of the film to people, and we were traveling all the time.

We felt like our job was really just to engage the communities that already care about the issues in our movie. That's a lot easier than trying to convince people to be interested in your film.

Caitlin Boyle: We did a lot of person-to-person contacting. We tried to hit people who had big membership networks, like Slow Food. I called them up, and chatted with the person who was head of membership. We just tried to think of people with connections. We also relied on Green List, which is a database of environmental organizations. We also had a list of CSAs [community-supported agriculture groups], and so we'd send e-mails and postcards to 10 or 20 farms in the area around where we were having a screening.

I did a lot of boring trolling on the Internet. We e-mailed restaurants who cared about sourcing local foods, and professors, and natural food people, and students who were leaders of environmental groups on campuses. Probably one-third of the people I e-mailed e-mailed back, offering to help us. And of those people, some had their own mailing list, some would put something up on a bulletin board in their store, or some would hand out flyers at the farmer's market.

> "We felt like our job was really just to engage the communities that already care about the issues in our movie. That's a lot easier than trying to convince people to be interested in your film."

If I saw that there was a post about *King Corn* on The Epicurean, or some other blog, I'd add them to my list of people to contact the next time something happened. So I'd e-mail them and say, "The DVD is coming out, and here's a JPEG of the artwork." They'd pretty much always mention it. Unlike newspapers and magazines, blogs seem to always be looking for content.

We didn't really have a standard e-mail. We'd offer people high-res images, posters, or postcards. It was really just about being personal. We tried to have it not feel corporate and studio-like. We just worked 15-hour days every day. We used the grassroots model.

Michael "Burnie" Burns
Creator of the Animated Series "Red vs. Blue"

After his first indie film project didn't turn him into the next Tarantino, Burnie Burns took a job at a tech support center in Austin, Texas. In 2003, along with some college friends and co-workers, he created the animated series "Red vs. Blue: The Blood Gulch Chronicles," which featured a wise-cracking cast of warriors from the Microsoft videogame "Halo." It quickly became the most popular (and long-running) machinima series on the Net. (Machinima uses environments and characters created by videogame rendering engines to tell new stories.) Eventually, Burns and his collaborators were able to quit their day jobs to work full time on "Red vs. Blue" – and its online store and community site. Graham Leggat, director of the San Francisco Film Society, describes the series as "part locker-room humor, part Beckett-like absurdist tragicomedy, part wicked vivisection of game culture..."

★ ★ ★ ★ ★

Our first series started April 1, 2003 and ran through 2007.

For us, getting noticed was pretty instantaneous. We put up the first two videos, and they got linked to by Fark and Slashdot [two sites about technology news]. With the techie humor, it was a good fit for them. Drew [Curtis, editor of Fark] linked to us every week for the whole first season. And after the fourth or fifth episode, I started to buy a banner ad on Fark, one of the hundred or so that rotates through the site. I paid maybe $100 for the week.

At the time, the only people doing video on the Internet were "Happy Tree Friends" and "Homestar Runner," it seemed. It wasn't like it is today, with this endless stream of video on the Web. Within the first month of "Red vs. Blue," we'd get 150,000 people watching a video. I think by Episode #7 or #8, we were at half a million. By the middle of that first season of 19 episodes, we were doing a full million downloads every time we put up a new video.

As people were coming to our site to watch the videos, we started making sure there was other cool stuff to do, other than just wait for the video to download. We started building more of a community site. That site now has 680,000 registered members. People would get involved in the discussion forums. Initially, people were talking about "Red vs. Blue," but then they'd branch out into other stuff - politics, movies, comics.

Everything we've done with traditional media never compared to getting mentioned on some Web site or some blog. We went on "TRL" on MTV, and we though it'd be perfect for our audience. You couldn't ask for

> "The first guy on our team quit his day job two months after the DVD came out."

better promotion. We wondered how we'd handle the traffic. We called up our Internet provider, and talked to them about adding more servers. Then we did the interview, and the needle just did not move. But a video gets linked on Fark or Digg, and watch out - people can just click the link and go to it.

Audience sponsorships. We created what we call sponsorships in the site, where you could donate $10 through PayPal or a check or money order. For a period of six months, we give those people access to higher-resolution videos. They see new episodes on Friday instead of Sunday. We put bonus content or extended content up for people who sponsor, and scripts. Those people are also identified on the site as our sponsors.

Then, once the first season was over, we produced a DVD. That was our first product. We stopped making new episodes for almost two months. We shipped the DVDs out ourselves, in our living rooms and garages, before we hired someone to do it for us.

The first guy on our team quit his day job two months after the DVD came out, in 2004. I was the last one to quit my day job. I'd been there for twelve years. I wanted to make sure other people got paid first, because I knew I was going to stay motivated doing what we were doing.

When we had the DVD, we got it into GameStop [a retail store that sells videogames]. We had a mutual friend who put us in contact with each other. They knew the product, and they liked it. Then, we got into Wal-Mart, the biggest seller of DVDs in the US. There are always these notions of, you can't do stuff. I wanted to prove that we could get ourselves into Wal-Mart without a distributor. We just called them directly. They said that they buy all their DVDs from this one manufacturer. So we talked to two or three different people who did placements in Wal-Mart, and went through one of those companies.

But most of our DVDs have been sold through our site. We also sold them at various comic conventions. We also do some special videos for [Microsoft's] Xbox Live Marketplace, and they sell them as downloads.

At the end of every video we make, there's a slate that says, "To see more videos, visit RedVsBlue.com," so the videos are advertisements for our site, and our store.

Other revenue sources. I think the #2 thing for us, in terms of revenue, would be t-shirts. We also do some contract work, like TV commercials that involve machinima.

People wanted to know how we made the videos, so we put up the "how you make machinima video" FAQ.

We go to about fifteen conventions a year. On Wednesday, I'm going to Melbourne and Sydney for film festivals.

We're totally happy. What we think is, if we can produce something on our own budget and stick it in this distribution model, which works, we'll look at TV and feature films when we get to a point where we want to do something that we just don't have the resources to do.

One piece of advice for people is about consistency. A lot of people put out one thing and it's really popular. They're surprised, and they don't have anything else to do. People really want consistent content. You can't go three or four months without something new.

We don't want to make videos over four minutes long. Anything over that, people just tune out.

Sandi DuBowski
Documentary Filmmaker

Sandi DuBowski's ambi-tions are encapsulated in the address of his Web site: FilmsThatChangetheWorld. com. His primary goal in making documentaries, he says, is social impact.

His first feature-length documentary, *Trembling Before G-d*, delved into the

world of Orthodox and Hasidic Jews who are gay or lesbian. The movie became the centerpiece of a campaign that included screenings at synagogues; a conference on homosexuality in Judaism; a "Fresh Air" interview with Terry Gross; hundreds of "town hall"-style screenings with discussions afterward; training facilitators in Israel to talk with teachers and principals in preparation for the film's television broadcast; and a sabbath celebration at the Sundance Film Festival. In 2007, DuBowski produced *A Jihad for Love*, a documentary about gay, lesbian, and transgender Muslims. (*Jihad* director Parvez Sharma is at left in the photo.) It premiered at the Toronto Film Festival.

★ ★ ★ ★ ★

I evaluate what I want to do by three criteria: social impact, revenue and prosperity, and building my career. When I think about anything, I ask, does it fulfill these criteria?

I want to use the Web to ask pressing questions about tolerance and dignity and respect and atonement. With *Trembling*, we created a Web site called FilmsThatChangetheWorld.com. I hired a digital outreach director to work on the site. I felt it was important to build an umbrella under which I could hang all my projects.

Everything took far too long. Things didn't work. It often seemed like it was at the brink of technical disaster. It cost probably $50,000 or more to build the Web site. The Fledgling Fund contributed some of that, and individual donors gave some.

House parties. For [the Jewish high holidays of] Rosh Hashanah and Yom Kippur, we created an interactive map on the site, and invited people to create their own DVD house parties to show *Trembling*. They could make it a private party for only people they knew, or a public party. We created 85 house parties in 16 countries. We built our own software to organize the house parties. We sold the DVDs for them directly through our Web site

I hired someone to do outreach to MySpace. He would reach out to Jewish gays and lesbians and send them friend requests for my "Films That Change the World" page on MySpace. We had a promotional video there for the house parties.

> "Most house parties, it turned out, were generated by people I knew or had met, and people that they knew. They did it because of personal connections."

But most house parties, it turned out, were generated by people I knew or had met, and people that they knew. They did it because of personal connections, and because they wanted to share the film with others. It wasn't like the magical social network of MySpace created action. Somehow, I don't think that MySpace is my audience, my crowd. I don't think it can lead to effective organizing.

Online shorts. I also created a series of short videos with Steven Greenberg, the Orthodox gay rabbi who is in *Trembling*. There were little teachable moments, and holiday videos. We put those on every single Web site we could find. I think people saw them, but I don't think they generated house parties or DVD sales, which is really the core thing.

On Facebook, people follow me there. They know that I opened *Jihad* in Toronto and LA. I created event listings for every city through Facebook, which Facebook users could sign up to attend. And that did seem to have some turn-out effect.

I've built myself as a brand. I've taken up the rock star touring model. That's why I signed up with a speaker's agency [Keppler Speakers] – it's a huge source of generating revenue. I did 800 live events with *Trembling*. I love doing Q&As after screenings and engaging with audiences.

The audience database. Collecting e-mail addresses is extremely important. I have about 18,000 e-mail addresses now. When I sell my DVD through Breakthrough Distribution and Neoflix, they give me the e-mail addresses of the purchasers. That's very valuable to me. If my speaking tour is coming to a school or university, or I have a new movie coming out, I can let people know.

I can't stand making a film and watching it die.

With *Jihad*, [director] Parvez [Sharma] blogged for the Huffington Post. We've featured a female Iranian blogger on our site. Our blog is sometimes the only way to reach our audiences, who can't see the film because of state power and censorship. But I should mention that we have passed copies of the DVD

> "The e-mail addresses of the [DVD] purchasers [are] very valuable to me. If...I have a new movie coming out, I can let people know."

into Muslim countries so they can have illegal house parties.

The big challenge is figuring out how do you create a connection between the online and the offline. Getting people to show up for a screening of your movie is a big deal.

Gregg and Evan Spiridellis
Co-Founders, JibJab Media

Gregg Spiridellis, a newly-minted MBA from the Wharton School of Business, and his brother Evan, an independent animator, started JibJab Media in 1999. For much of its early history, the Brooklyn micro-studio was "on the verge of bankruptcy and running out of cash," in Evan's words. (That's Evan on the right.) But in 2004, the brothers had an online (and offline) hit with the political satire "This Land," and since then they've had a string of wildly-successful animated videos, including "Good to Be in DC" and "Time for Some Campaigning," and their now-traditional year-in-review videos. Their work has premiered several times on the "Tonight Show." They've collaborated with Disney on a holiday book; director John Landis on a sketch comedy contest; and Weird Al Yankovic. Their studio, now based in Venice, California, employs 35 people. Their primary business is now "social programming" – creating customizable content for special occasions like birthdays and anniversaries – though they still produce several original videos each year.

★ ★ ★ ★ ★

Gregg Spiridellis: When we got started, in 1999, three things were happening. The cost of producing high-quality content was plummeting. The capital investment in equipment was no longer a barrier to entry. You had great artists like Evan and his friends making films with off-the-shelf technology.

Second was the opening of distribution. The Internet let you reach anyone on the planet, even if we were a little bright-eyed and bushy-tailed about what was possible with 56k dial-up modems.

The third thing was that, since we could capture e-mail addresses, we could build an on-going relationship with the audience, and build a brand.

Evan Spiridellis: Even in 1999, there was always a box that said "Subscribe" or "Enter your e-mail here," on everything we did.

GS: We didn't know the term viral back then, but we knew people were e-mailing stuff to friends, and we knew that having peoples' e-mail addresses would make it easier to propagate new content releases.

We bootstrapped the company in Brooklyn, basically producing e-cards with Shockwave [early multi-media technology for the Web], making enough money to fund the original productions, building our list, and just getting the work out there. In February of 2000, we had the "Founding Fathers Rap," which became a cult Internet hit. Then in November of 2000, we had our first mainstream hit with "Capitol Ill," which was about George W. Bush and Al Gore having a rap battle. It got coverage on CNN, but it was still pretty niche. Most people still weren't consuming video entertainment online. It was probably seen about five million times.

ES: It also got licensed by "MadTV," which aired on Fox, and they played it right before the election.

GS: We were doing deals with AtomFilms, licensing our original content to them for use on the Web. Our shop got up to 13 people.

Then, in 2001, the dot-com bust wiped out all of our clients. Our licensing business went away. The ad business deteriorated. It went down to just the two of us. We packed the studio into a U-Haul, and drove across the country. We knew we wanted to be at the beach.

We set up shop, and just kept plugging away. It was a nuclear winter for online content. We did a toy line, and children's books. In August 2003, we did the video "Ahnold for Governor," which was a nice little hit for us. It was in Sundance's digital competition. We didn't submit it; they contacted us.

ES: Any time we would make money, we would funnel it into our original productions. We had an e-mail list of maybe about 120,000 people.

GS: We were learning what works. We knew we wanted to do comedy, but we started discovering that people liked stuff with music, stuff that had to do with politics, stuff that was topical.

But by 2004, we were starting to wonder if we were gonna have to get real jobs.

Then, in July of that year, we released "This Land." We mailed our 120,000 subscribers about it. Suddenly, we were doing 500,000 views a day. At the time, our site was on a shared server in Texas. It was like that moment in *Jaws*: we knew we needed a bigger boat.

I think it was the most effective $400 marketing campaign in history. It showed that if you have a relatively small, hard-core fan base, you can get exponential growth out of them if the content is really relevant.

The bleed-over to traditional media was unbelievable. We were guests on the "Tonight Show," and "Persons of the Week" on ABC News. That kind of drove more online adoption. And we were always capturing peoples' e-mails.

> "At 10 PM on the day [our video] played on 'The Tonight Show,' Evan mocked up a DVD cover in PhotoShop, and I set up a Yahoo Store."

We did a licensing deal with Yahoo for some original productions. That gave us a little capital.

We released another video that October, "Good to be in DC," that premiered on the "Tonight Show." At 10 PM on the day that played on "The Tonight Show," Evan mocked up a DVD cover in PhotoShop, and I set up a Yahoo Store. The "Today Show" was coming the next day to talk to us, and we wanted to mention that we were selling our stuff on DVDs. During that interview, we held up the fake DVD and mentioned that we were selling them. We sold 100,000 DVDs. We told people they wouldn't ship for six weeks, but we wound up making them in four. It was $10 for less than four minutes of content.

We also sold downloads for people who wanted to play the videos in full-screen, high-resolution. We sold them through our own online store, without DRM [digital rights management], for $1.99.

ES: It was definitely the "Today Show" that moved most of the DVDs, but there was one day when we went to a bunch of satellite studios, like Fox and MSNBC, and at every interview, we lifted up this fake DVD.

Our e-mail list went from 130,000 to 500,000 really quick, and in the two years after "This Land," we got to 700,000. Today, it's just over four million people.

GS: How often do we e-mail? Once a month is a pretty good guide. Twice a month in December, which is the high season for us. We don't just mail in order to mail, and drive traffic, because we get an unbelievable response rate on our list.

ES: We don't want to annoy people. We only reach out when we have something valuable for them, something we're really proud of. For e-mailing we use Lyris, which is an e-mail list manager. We've used that forever. It's a hosted service.

GS: Today, the way we get people to sign up now for membership, and to be on our list, is that when you want to create a "Starring You" movie, where images of you and your friends are in the video, you need to register for our site and give us your e-mail, so that you can upload your head and save your movies and share them.

ES: We also created a subscription, and benefits solely for subscribers. It costs $19.95 a year, and you can send unlimited e-cards, and get access to new content first.

GS: In 2000, back in Brooklyn, I used to check the in-bound e-mails, and we always responded. One time I got an e-mail from a kid who said, "I want to make cartoons. How do you do it?" I sent him some links. A couple months later, he wrote back and said, "My mommy wants to make a children's book. Can you guys draw the pictures?" We said, "Have her give us a call." She was a music producer working on a book with LL Cool J. He came out to our studio and we wound up doing a children's book, *And the Winner Is...* with him.

ES: Now, we have two people on operations who handle all the e-mail. But if we get questions from students getting started in animation, I talk to anybody. I have an e-mail exchange or a phone call. It doesn't cost much to be nice or responsive, and when I was just out of school, I needed all the advice I could get. You treat people the way you want to be treated. Our whole business is dependent on our audience, and we take that really seriously.

GS: We get 500 in-bound e-mails a day. I look at them as an RSS feed. While I'm waiting for lunch, I use the Google Reader on my iPhone to scan through them.

After "This Land" came out, our business model was to license content to people like Yahoo. Video didn't move around; it tended to stay in one place. Then YouTube came along and blew up that idea. You couldn't control video anymore. It forced us to say, "OK, the original JibJab videos that we produce are no longer how we're gonna make revenue. They're a marketing opportunity."

At first, we thought that advertising would be the way we'd go. But the more we looked at that, we realized that even if every video we made reached five million people, which is a baseline for us – "Time for Some Campaigning" is over 15 million now – that would generate $100,000 in ad revenue in the best case. And we're spending about $75,000 to make the videos. Where's the profit, where's the scale?

ES: And if you even have a near-miss instead of a real hit, you're in the red.

GS: In 2006, we came to the realization that an ad model wasn't going to cut it. We'd taken venture capital money at that point.

We happened to look at American Greetings' financials. They're a public company. They have an $85 million business in online greeting cards. We said, "This is content. We do content."

But Evan said, "There's no f***ing way I'm making JibJab an e-card company."

ES: But just because the bar was so low with e-cards didn't mean it had to stay there.

GS: We felt we could create new expectations, new formats.

ES: And we're also innovating our production model, creating a virtual studio. We look at blogs, and see that talent is everywhere. We might find a great writer in New York, and a voice guy in San Francisco, and an artist in Italy. Our job is to pull together these creative SWAT teams. A two or three or four-person team can produce great content, and they share in the revenue that gets generated by that content.

GS: We have fan pages on Facebook and MySpace, but we don't really use them for audience aggregation. If we can get people on our site, we have much more flexibility with how we can communicate with them. We do use something called Gigya for widget distribution, which allows you to publish content from JibJab to any of the social networks. But if we were starting JibJab today, I'd definitely be making social networks a big part of what we do.

> "The idea that we're going to hit some sort of steady model is a false hope. ...We've had forty business models in nine years."

The idea that we're going to hit some sort of steady model is a false hope. You've just got to keep moving. We've had forty business models in nine years. I don't see it slowing down at all.

ES: We had pitched a feature film to a major studio, right before we raised venture capital money. It was green-lit. But we were asking ourselves, "Do we want to go forward and be Evan and Gregg, these two creators working with a studio, or do we want to build something bigger, like a Disney or a Henson?"

We are just fiercely independent guys. You take studio money, and as much as they love you, you're working for somebody. If they say, "Make those purple shoes red," well, you've got a boss. And with JibJab, we got used to going directly to our audience.

GS: We innovate, we produce, we release, we get the response. The idea of spending two or three years on one thing, and not knowing how much support it would get when it was released – it just didn't feel like the right time.

Timo Vuorensola
Science Fiction Director & Collaboration Pioneer

Throughout the 1990s, a group of friends in Finland turned out a series of animated and live action "Star Trek" parodies under the banner "Star Wreck." The sixth installment, *Star Wreck: In the Pirkinning*, was the first made as a full-length feature, and the first to come up with a new approach to collaboration that invited people across the Internet to contribute 3-D models, digital environments, acting performances, and even the film's score. Much of the production took place in a converted two-room apartment, the kitchen of which had been converted into a render farm. The total budget, not including sponsored and in-kind goods and services, was about $20,000.

Timo Vuorensola was the director, shepherding the project along over seven years. He's now directing another collaboratively-produced project, *Iron Sky*, about a group of Nazis who escaped to the moon during World War II and are about to return to earth. Vuorensola also helped launch the site Wreck A Movie, which offers a platform that allows other filmmakers to get their audiences involved.

The Internet is a collection of communities. You need to create a community around your film. That will not happen if you keep things to yourself. You need to open yourself up, show your face, show your production, let people get inside. People do a lot of things when they get enthusiastic about something. They help the production, give money, or run into the streets and scream about your production. You need to allow people to do that. It's an enormous viral force.

I don't know if it was luck or if we did something right, but we were able to create a pretty big community around *Star Wreck: In the Pirkinning*, and another one is building up around our current project, *Iron Sky*.

The beginning. We started to work on *Star Wreck* in 1998. We went around to different forums and posted about it, so people knew what we were doing. Some of that was on a "Star Trek" board. We'd say, "We're gonna go out and make this film. Does anybody want to help?" At first, no one does. But over time, if you do some things on your own that really show quality, and show who you are, people want to feel helpful. They sense that there is one guy behind this, and he needs our help.

When a big film enters a community, no one believes they're actually going to need help.

We had made five "Star Wreck" movies by ourselves. With the sixth, we had a script, and we said, "OK, we're going to need ten or twenty people on the Internet to read it and comment on it, and send ideas."

Community contributions. After we had the script right, we realized we'd need a big fleet of spacecraft. None of us were able to do modeling; we could do animation, but not modeling. We started to go around the Internet looking for Web sites that had to do with 3-D modeling, and we said, "We're working on this cool film. Would you like to help us?" A lot of people already had models of spacecraft that they wanted to make better.

We found actors on the Internet, too. But we said, "We need you to come to Finland for the shoot." People came from Japan, from Canada, from the States, from Norway. We found the musician who did the whole score on the Internet. He just dropped us his new music, and we went back and forth on instant messenger with changes.

In 2005, when the film came out, people started to do their own fan-subtitled versions. It was a Finnish language film with English subtitles when we released it. But it got translated into about thirty different languages.

Star Wreck was made by a core group of five people, but over 300 people are credited in the end credits, and there was a larger community of 3000 who were involved in some way. They evangelized *Star Wreck* in whatever channels they could. They contacted local press. They took the film under their wings.

We decided not to create a media kit. We should have done one. We would've gotten better media coverage.

The total amount of money we spent was around 15,000 Euros. And we made that money back, ten or twenty times over.

DVD distribution, and other deals. We sold distribution rights to television. It was shown on TV in Finland, Japan, Italy, and Belgium, along with some other places. It had a big merchandising element, with t-shirts and caps. We printed them ourselves. It cost about two Euros per shirt, and we sold them for twenty Euros.

The bulk of the money came from us selling the DVD ourselves. We also did a distribution deal with Universal Pictures for retail sales of the DVD in Scandinavia, which came out a year-and-a-half after the original release. But we made more money selling it ourselves.

I should mention that it was initially released for free on the Internet, in October 2005, as a Torrent file and as a direct download. Later, we released it on YouTube and Google Video. Selling DVDs despite the free version is a funny thing, but people do it anyway. I think you can double your income if you give something away for free. I don't believe in piracy. It's just people using the available technology.

You need to offer different monetization options for different customers. Some people watch it on the Web for twenty minutes and then want to buy the DVD. Some people watch the whole film on BitTorrent, but then want to support us by buying merchandise. We want to let you give us money in any possible way.

War bonds. With *Iron Sky*, we're selling 2000 of what we call "war bonds," which cost 50 Euros. You get a DVD of the teaser trailer, and a little booklet about the film, and a certificate that says you participated in the fight against space Nazis. They're selling OK, but it's not a way to finance the whole film. Just a way for people to support us.

This new film is even more collaborative than *Star Wreck*. We have a couple thousand active people, and the film will be out in 2010.

This is my day job now, every day since early in 2006. I used to work in telemarketing before that.

Those who will survive all of these big changes in the filmmaking industry are those who know how to activate the community – in production, in distribution, in PR, in everything. It's a force that not everyone knows how to gather.

Steve Garfield
Videoblogger

Steve Garfield helped meld the mediums of blogging and cinema verité video reportage, which yielded vlogging. He has been a correspondent and contributor to the satirical news series "Rocket-boom," political analysis site techPresident, and TheUptake, a site for citizen journalism. He created "Vlog Soup," a show that surveys the best of videoblogs, and teaches a course called "New Media Tools for Journalism" at Boston University. Garfield is often sought out by tech companies to test new cameras, phones, and Web services, and he earns a living as a consultant helping clients understand the world of Internet video.

★ ★ ★ ★ ★

I gravitate towards doing things that are fun.

On January 1st, 2004, I integrated video into my blog for the first time. I did it as a New Year's resolution.

The power of the link. All of the early vloggers [video bloggers] linked to one another, and helped each other build an audience. The Wall Street *Journal*, the New York *Times*, and *Time* magazine would cover vlogging, but they didn't include links. It did nothing for my site's traffic.

There was a videoblogging group on Yahoo, and as people wanted to learn how to do it, they joined. We all discussed how to do things, and watched each others' videos. In 2004, the group was maybe 40 or 50 people. In 2005, I helped organize the first Vloggercon, in New York City. It was an "unconference" that brought together a lot of the people who'd gotten into videoblogging to share advice and talk about tools.

Free advice. The way I meet people and get most of my jobs is offering to help people. That's my method of operation. When "Rocketboom" [a satirical video series] first came out, I critiqued their first video, minute by minute. Amanda [Congdon, the host,] threw some papers, and it was funny. I said, "Do more of that." We started e-mailing, and then we met. I became one of their first correspondents. At the opening of my reports, I'd always say, "Hi, I'm Steve Garfield from SteveGarfield.com." And Amanda would mimic that. It really worked for me.

Now, the thing I'm doing is live video broadcasts, from this Nokia N82 phone directly to the Internet. [The company sent Garfield the phone for free as part of its "blogger relations" program.] Right now, I use a service called Qik for sending video from the phone to the Web. My Twitter followers get a message whenever I'm broadcasting live, and people can text me on the phone and do things like ask me to ask a particular question of someone that I'm with.

> "I'm always attracted to what's new. I like to jump on it, test it out, and then share what I find."

How do I make a living? I go around the country and speak, and I produce video for clients. I get paid to create online video for companies like Legal Sea Foods, a food site called SpicesofLife.com, a non-profit called Third Sector New England, and Boston City Councillor John Tobin. He was the first elected official in the US to vlog, and he has me on retainer. I often get paid to speak, and to teach. "Rocketboom" pays a little stipend.

The lure of the new. I Twitter three or four times a day. On my "About Me" page, it says, "Follow me on Twitter." I think people follow me because I sometimes go to interesting places, talk to cool people, link to lots of sites and videos.

I'm always attracted to what's new. I like to jump on it, test it out, and then share what I find.

Robert Greenwald
Documentary Filmmaker

If most filmmakers try to advance their careers by getting the green light to make movies that are longer, more expensive, and involve bigger crews, Robert Greenwald has been heading in the opposite direction. Greenwald has spent much of his career directing made-for-TV dramas like *The Burning Bed*, features like *Steal This Movie!*, and more recently, documentaries about Fox News and Wal-Mart. He has been nominated for 25 Emmy Awards and two Golden Globes.

But starting in the thick of the 2008 Presidential campaign, Greenwald turned to making short videos and distributing them on the Web. One focused on Senator John McCain's inability to recall how many homes he owned. More recently, he has produced videos about the real estate crash and excessive Wall Street bonuses.

Greenwald has set up a foundation, Brave New Foundation, so that donors can support his politically-charged video initiatives. He has one million subscribers to his e-mail list, and his collection of YouTube videos has amassed more than 35 million views. Greenwald has also raised money for feature films over the Internet, and sought help on his projects from a far-flung network of collaborators.

★ ★ ★ ★ ★

Scott Kirsner: So many filmmakers are still trapped by the idea that to be important and to matter in the world, you have to make a 90-minute or two-hour long film. You've kind of gone off on this track of making shorter things for the Web.

Robert Greenwald: We did have an a-ha moment. I'd finished the film *Iraq for Sale*, which is about war profiteering. We took a little piece, based on an ad that Halliburton had out. We hacked their ad, changed it around, and used it to tell people to watch *Iraq for Sale*. We put it on this new thing called YouTube. In three days, there were 11,000 views. I was staggered. People found it, and we didn't do anything.

With our political documentaries, we can do them faster than anybody. But that could be nine months, or eight months of working 24/7. That's too long. With a three- or five-minute piece, we were shrinking the [production] time.

We made a decision at that point that we were going to try to fundraise, try to do the short piece. This wonderful group of funders, the Democracy Alliance, came forth and gave us the support. We had projected two million views for our first year. We hit 11 million, and now we're at 35 or 36 million.

SK: Is that every year?

RG: No, since we started.

SK: The MoveOn.org partnership, when you were first getting started making these very activist documentaries, seems like it was really key, where they gave you access to their members list. Were there other partnerships that were important?

RG: Well, MoveOn never lent me the list. The first film, *Uncovered*, was about the reasons that we'd been given for the [Iraq] war. That's something that MoveOn was politically interested in. If I'd come to them with a movie about Darfur, their membership wouldn't have been engaged. It wouldn't have made sense.

Going forward, I'd discuss the projects in advance with them, before I even started. With *Outfoxed* [which indicted Fox News' approach to journalism], it was a combination of Wes Boyd's and John Podesta's idea – we were at a conference brainstorming. [Boyd is a founder of MoveOn.org, and Podesta is a former Clinton official who now runs the Center for American Progress, a Washington think tank.]

People think you make a film and then you go to a group and say, "Will you distribute it?" Well, they're not distributors.

SK: So they didn't lend you the list, but they did promoted *Uncovered*.

RG: Because it was about issues that they and their members were working on politically.

SK: Most of your funding these days comes from non-profits like the Democracy Alliance? You're not relying on individual donors as much?

RG: It has four parts. There are the small individual donors who give us $50 or $10 a month, or $100 when they see something they like. Foundations. High net worth individuals. And groups with similar perspectives to ours, where they will engage our online expertise to help tell the stories they need told.

SK: So there still is that channel for individuals to give $20?

RG: Yes. That's critical. We have 6,000 or 7,000 people who give us $10 a month – varying amounts. Each piece of those four parts is important.

SK: Tell me a bit about how you think about the audience differently these days, versus the days when you were making made-for-TV movies or theatrical films. That was kind of a one-way communication, right?

RG: In general, this audience has very strong opinions. If they don't like what you do, you'll hear from them. Or if they do like what you do, you hear from them. I find that absolutely wonderful.

The audience votes with their 'forward' button. If they see a video that they think has something to say, they forward it. All the money in the world and all the king's horses can't get them to do that. In that sense, it's truly the free market. Just think about it – what are the chances you're going to forward a video to a friend or a relative or a colleague if it doesn't grab you?

> "The audience votes with their 'forward' button. If they see a video that they think has something to say, they forward it."

Maybe one of the greatest things about our audience is that they really want to learn something. If we do stuff where it doesn't give them something new, it never does as well. Like, who knew about the connections between Burger King and Goldman Sachs? [Goldman Sachs, a major shareholder in the fast food chain, got a $6.5 billion government bailout and paid executives millions in bonuses, while the average Burger King worker earns $14,000 a year.]

SK: The last time I visited you, you were telling me about how you found collaborators all over the world to do research and shoot second-unit footage for *Iraq for Sale*. Tell me a little bit about the state of collaboration today, in terms of opening it up to people beyond these walls?

RG: We've made a commitment to put a lot of resources into two arms of Brave New Films. One is video activists. We want to have 5,000 people around the country who can go film SEIU [the Service Employees International Union] at a Burger King, or go film someone who is losing their home. Their material will come in to us, and we'll post it. We want to be able to hit a button, by ZIP code or by state, and really have them involved. And we want to have 5,000 people who are video distributors – who understand that they are Paramount Studios, they are CBS. If they take our video and get it to 100 people, that's hugely important.

SK: Are you going to give these video creators any directions?

RG: Oh, yeah. We'll be very specific. On our "Fighting for Our Homes" campaign, you'll see that there are 30 or 35 videos from people who've lost their homes. Some of those were Skype or iChat or video cameras that people send in to us.

SK: What's new that you're especially energized by these days?

RG: I'm very intrigued with Twitter. I have no idea where it's going to go, but I'm enjoying it. There's information and articles and links, and people doing things I'd never know about. I do it myself. I don't have anyone doing it for me. How we'll use it is up for grabs.

From a story-telling point of view, we've experimented a little bit with series or Webisodes. I think there are opportunities there now – we call them campaigns. We'll be doing a series of videos around "Enemies of Change," a whole thing around Afghanistan. How they play out as individual pieces and how you put them together is going to be interesting.

We also have our own little studio, in the barbershop next door where I used to get my hair cut. It's two-and-a-half people now, and you can reach millions with it. It can look every bit as good as MSNBC or CNN.

M dot Strange
Animator

In 2006, before he'd finished his first feature-length film, *We Are the Strange,* animator M dot Strange had already started posting a series of video "production diary" clips to YouTube – mostly featuring him talking directly to the camera from his bedroom/studio in San Jose, California. He followed that with a series of "Film Skool" videos, sharing what he'd learned from the three years he'd spent blending stop-motion, anime, green screens, and a twisted, post-apocalyptic creative vision.

None of the videos individually was a break-out hit, but Strange managed to attract a loyal YouTube audience of a few thousand viewers. Then, in a late-2006 post titled "Mega Hella Major News!", he told his YouTube fans that *We Are the Strange* had been accepted into the Sundance Film Festival. He later self-distributed the DVD through Film Baby, and in April 2008 released it in its entirety to YouTube (with a link encouraging viewers to buy the DVD.)

He earned enough from the release to dig himself out of the debt he'd incurred making *We Are the Strange* and also to fund his next project, *Heartstring Marionette.*

★ ★ ★ ★ ★

Now anybody can make a movie. But not everybody is going to be able to use this new model to find an audience and be successful.

When people ask me about attracting people to your stuff online, I don't know what to tell them, other than, "Be more interesting."

Inside the process. I think I'm a new type of entertainer. People watch my videos for the story of how I work, my creative process, even if they've never seen the movie. But some people online, their personal story overpowers the film, or the project they're working on. You've got to get people excited about both. You've got to be like a carny: crafty and resourceful.

A lot of the "making of" documentaries that studios produce for DVDs simply say, "We use a lot of proprietary stuff." They don't tell you how it's done. The doors are closed. But I've found that educational stuff can attract an audience. Share your techniques, and tell people about the software you're using. You're almost giving them the DVD extras before they buy the DVD.

When I started to make *We Are the Strange*, I kept a blog, but no one read it. I wrote every other day. I knew that I had to have something, but people didn't start reading it until my videos took off on YouTube.

Help from YouTube. I e-mailed the guys at YouTube, and they featured the trailer for my film. Within five days, it had 500,000 views. More than half the messages I got from YouTube were about how people could buy the film. Maybe it wasn't a good idea to have the trailer get seen so much before the film was out, or available on DVD. But I collected thousands of addresses.

I responded to all of the YouTube comments on my trailer, any person who had a question. You have to bridge that gap. You can't be to cool for it. As fast as someone becomes your fan, they can become someone posting everywhere and saying you suck. But if you respond to them, they become powerful. They're like bees, spreading your message.

If I made a video and I said I was sick, or that my computer broke, people would e-mail me and they were really concerned.

My persona online is about 70 percent me. He's this real person, and he shows all his flaws. He's a little bit censored – he's PG-13, where I am not. All I do is turn my webcam on. There are no titles, no editing.

Integrating the audience. While I was making the film, I asked the audience for photos, and I turned them into ghouls using PhotoShop, and I put them into a few shots as extras. When I was promoting the film, we'd have costume contests on YouTube. I said, "Dress up like a character from the movie, and I'll send you a signed poster. "

When people would put up fan videos related to me or the film on YouTube, I might comment on them, or mention it in my next video, or add it to my favorite videos list.

> "I asked the audience for photos, and I turned them into ghouls using PhotoShop, and I put them into a few shots as extras."

I submitted the film to the Sundance Film Festival, and I made sure to point out to the programmers there that I had built up this following on YouTube. When I got in, I posted a video on YouTube where I played the voicemail message from them, that *We Are the Strange* would be screened at Sundance in January 2007. I said, "I've got to finish it by then."

With the YouTube audience, it was good for me to be able to see what they're into, how they talk, where they go to. My fans are mostly male, and mostly under 25. Some of the dialogue and terminology in *We Are the Strange* incorporates Internet slang from these kids on YouTube, and videos they made. Watching what they watch, and listening to songs on their MySpace pages is a little bit like market research, and a little bit like stalking. I used music from a fan's MySpace page in one of my trailers, from the band Rabbit Junk.

I did a deal with Film Baby to sell a two-DVD set of the movie. Film Baby sells online and also does retail sales through a partnership with Rykodisc. Probably 95 percent of my income from the film came from selling DVDs – $15,000 from online sales through Film Baby's site, and $30,000 from retail DVD sales, though Ryko takes all these distribution fees on retail, which shaves off like 15 or 20 percent. I earned about $1,000 from merchandise and DVDs that I sold to fans face-to-face, and about $1000 from YouTube's partner program. I was about $10,000 in the hole from *We Are the Strange*. My new film will cost about $15,000. So I broke even, and funded the new film.

Piracy. Half my audience probably got *We Are the Strange* in a pirated form, through file-sharing. But they're an audience.

The less soul your creation has, the more commercial it will seem, and the more people will pirate it. Otherwise, people will find the artists and entertainers they like, and we'll go back to the days where you had patrons. People don't have to pay. They have to want to pay and support you.

We Are the Strange is available online in 17 different languages now. All the subtitles were done in less than two weeks. My audience did it, and I sent them autographed DVDs as a thank-you.

The band Mindless Self Indulgence saw my trailer, and I eventually sent them the DVD of the movie. They asked me to make a music video for their song "Animal." Some of my fans are now my collaborators. There's a 14-year old who is now better at 3-D modeling than me. I found six people from my YouTube audience – like 14 to 19-year-olds – to help with Flash animation, though I did about 95 percent of it. [All of M dot's collaborators got credit.]

> "You just have to innovate in the face of adversity. Creativity is free. In Hollywood, they solve any problem by throwing money at it."

For the independent person, you just have to innovate in the face of adversity. Creativity is free. In Hollywood, they solve any problem by throwing money at it.

I got offers from Hollywood. "Do you want to make a live-action G.I. Joe movie? Or a ninja movie in the style of *300*?" But I'm trying to avoid the grinder of doing other peoples' films. I think the edges get worn off your ideas. It kills your inspiration.

My next movie is *Heartstring Marionette*, a samurai movie. I posted the production schedule on my blog. It'll be out in 2010.

My idea of success is the ability to make your films your way, and share them with people all over the world. That's success.

Jonathan Coulton
Singer-Songwriter

In August 2005, when Jonathan Coulton quit his job as a software developer, he posted an entry on his blog titled "Don't Quit Your Day Job." "Part of me is sure this is exactly the right thing to do, while the rest of me is screaming that this is probably the dumbest thing I've ever done," he wrote.

Shortly after that, the Brooklyn-based singer-songwriter started a project to record and post one new song every week – a mix of originals and a few covers. He dubbed it "Thing a Week." In Week #4, he invited his fans to submit their own eight-bar solo for a song called "Shop Vac," and let the community decide which one they liked best for inclusion in the final version. In Week #5, his searching and introspective cover of Sir Mix-a-Lot's "Baby Got Back" took off like Internet wildfire.

Coulton has experimented with free downloads, karaoke versions of his songs, ringtones, and a system called "Demand It" that allows fans in various cities to request that he play shows there. He has also had fans produce books, animations, and videos based on his work. In 2009, he told me he was earning as much from his musical career as he'd ever earned at his old day job.

★ ★ ★ ★ ★

I played drums in school, in the marching band and jazz band. But then I picked up the guitar because it was cool, it was portable, and it was better for getting girls. I wrote angst-ridden songs about being a teenager, of course, and also some goofball songs – like a song about the lunch lady at school. At Yale, I was a music major, and I sang in the Whiffenpoofs, an *a capella* group that goes back a hundred years.

I moved to New York after school to be a musician. I was an assistant to an A&R guy in a division of EMI. I did a lot of temping. I was a beta tester for Ensoniq keyboards, playing them and reporting on bugs. I worked at an espresso bar on the Upper East Side, dealing with people who hadn't had their coffee yet. Then, after Ensoniq laid me off, I got a job with a software company that was owned by a friend of a friend. I was hired to answer phones, but eventually moved into programming.

A series of little breaks. A friend of mine from Yale, [the writer] John Hodgman, started a series of shows called the Little Gray Book Lectures in Brooklyn. Each one had a theme, like "Secrets of the Secret Agents," or "How to Gamble and Win." I'd write a song for each one, like "Gambler's Prayer." It helped me find my songwriting style, this combination of funny and sad. I put out my first CD of songs from the Little Gray Books series, recorded at home on my PC, and mastered by a friend. Being part of the series also got me invited to PopTech, this technology conference up in Maine. I got a standing ovation there, during my song "Mandelbrot Set." That's when I felt I had really found something – found my audience.

Literally, the minute I got off the stage, I realized what an idiot I was. I had just pressed some CDs, but I had no Web site. Well, I had the domain, but the only thing there was a picture of my goatee. I went backstage at PopTech and used some laptop in the green room and put on some links to my songs, and a message: "Soon you'll be able to buy my CD." At the next PopTech, the following year, I brought my five-song CD and I had a Web site that was more real.

I got asked to write some songs for a special issue of the magazine *Popular Science*. And then a producer for MTV asked me to write a theme song for a show called "Social History."

I was starting to remember that I'd come to New York to be a musician, and I felt myself slipping into a career as a software developer. It was a good job – upper five figures. It was really comfortable in some ways. It took me a long time to reverse the trend.

Ditching the day job. Everything in the music business told me that I needed to play more shows, be fifteen years younger, and not have glasses. I needed to be a young, dedicated, good-looking artist with a known quantity of reachable fans.

But I left my job in September of 2005. I started "Thing a Week" shortly after that – writing and recording and posting one song every week, which made me feel like I had some kind of structure to my weeks. I did that for a year, through September of 2006.

At the start, it wasn't clear to me that I was going to be able to make money. I thought I might have to go back and get a day job. Initially, I tried things like putting a tip jar on the site, or selling a $1 per week voluntary "subscription" to Thing a Week.

> "My goal was really just to make a living by making music and putting it on the Internet."

Over the course of that first year, I had many ups and downs. It felt great, and it felt like it wasn't going to work. My goal was really just to make a living by making music and putting it on the Internet. By 2007, I was making about 40 percent of my income from selling MP3s, and the rest of it is split pretty evenly between ticket sales at shows, and sales of physical things like CDs and t-shirts.

Audience-driven booking. "Demand It" on the site Eventful was incredibly useful when I was first starting. You can put something on your site that says, "Sign up here and tell me where you live, if you want me to perform in your city." I can log in and see all of the cities where people are demanding me.

I was on tour with [author and "Daily Show" performer] John Hodgman in Seattle. We had an event on Friday. I sent a message out to all the people in Seattle who'd demanded me, and posted on my blog saying, "I'm going to be in Seattle, and I'd be happy to do a show on Saturday night if I can find a venue." This was maybe a week-and-a-half before the date. Within 24 hours, I got five or six responses from people, some who'd actually called up venues to find out who the booker was. One guy owned a coffee shop, and he offered that as a venue. The one that looked like the best option was the Jewelbox Theater at the Rendezvous. It held about 75 people, and there were 75 people there. That's when it all clicked for me.

Before that, I'd called up a booking agent and asked him how you get shows lined up. He said, "Well, you play in your city first, because that doesn't cost anything. You build up a following. Then, if you have a car, you can drive to nearby cities, and you start doing these ever-widening concentric circles to make your following bigger and bigger."

But after that Seattle event, he called me up and said, "Forget everything I said. What you just did is a whole new thing."

From that point on, he decided to be my booking agent. He and I would look at the numbers on Demand It. We'd had 45 demands in Seattle, and that turned in to a 75-person audience. Then, we tried San Francisco. For me, it holds true that the audience size will be larger than the number of people who've made demands. Demand It has helped my agent sell me to venues who've never heard of me. He can say, "Look, we just did a show in San Francisco, and the demands were at this level, and this many people showed up."

We've tried doing cities where the Demand It numbers just weren't there, because they were between two other cities where I was playing, and it hasn't worked.

With Demand It, while I don't have direct access to peoples' e-mail addresses, they do have a dashboard where you can say, "Show me how many people are demanding me within 75 miles of Atlanta," and then send a message to that group if you are performing there.

The 'Portal' theme. A fan of mine was the head of a development team at a videogame company, and she asked me if I'd write a song for the game "Portal." It wasn't really lucrative, but it was a huge amount of exposure. The song is called "Still Alive," and a character in the game sings it at the end of the game. I got to play the game and talk to all the writers while it was in development. The game was fantasic, and people really loved the song. That was by far the hugest exposure spike of my career. [On YouTube, several amateur musicians have posted videos of their own covers of "Still Alive."]

I have such direct access to my fans that advertising a show in traditional ways is mostly not necessary. But most venues do advertise anyway, just 'cause they're used to doing that. My shows sort of sell themselves. I have the blog, with maybe 6,000 active subscribers. I have a mailing list of about 8,000 people. I have 14,000 or 15,000 people following me on Twitter. And I publish my performances through all of those channels.

One really big thing for me is the derivative works that people have created, using my music. Everything I do is under a Creative Commons license. [Creative Commons allows more re-use and remixing than a traditional copyright.] People have made videos using "World of Warcraft" characters and put them on YouTube. Some of the videos have been seen millions of times. I don't know how you could even buy that kind of exposure, and I got it for free.

I have a live concert DVD that will be coming out soon, and I'm trying an experiment – I've hooked up with a distributor who will put it into retail stores. We'll see how that works.

Digital distribution. I do two different kinds of downloads. One is the downloads on my own Web site, where I use E-Junkie, which works with PayPal. I signed up with PayPal micropayments, which has a different commission structure if items are under $12, so if someone buys a single song, it's not the usual commission of like 30 cents plus some percentage for them. I'm not sure how well they publicize that micropayments offering. [Sellers pay five percent of the transaction, plus five cents.]

The other kind of download is digital distribution through CD Baby. They sell through iTunes, Emusic, Amazon

> "I sell more through CD Baby than I do through my own Web site, but I make more money through my own site."

MP3, and Rhapsody, and the split there is generally 70 percent to me, 30 percent to them. I sell more through CD Baby than I do through my own Web site, but I make more money through my own Web site.

I'm fully subsisting off being a 100 percent, full-time musician. I've been making enough money the last couple years that I'm not ashamed – I'm a contributing member of my family, even if I'm not becoming incredibly wealthy. But I'm doing about as well as I'd be doing if I had stayed at the software company where I used to work.

But I would not be making a good living if I were in a band with three other guys. And that's a real limitation of this method.

Damian Kulash
Singer and Guitarist, OK Go

The Chicago rock band OK Go got together in 1998, and released their debut album in 2002 on Capitol Records. They toured with They Might Be Giants and the National Public Radio show "This American Life," and licensed their songs for use in videogames, but the band suddenly achieved global fame in 2006 with two low-budget music videos distributed through YouTube. In the first, "A Million Ways," the band performed a tongue-in-cheek dance routine in the back yard of lead singer Damian Kulash. In the second, "Here It Goes Again," they danced on six moving treadmills. Both videos inspired fans to produce and post their own versions, and helped land the band on "Good Morning America" and The MTV Music Awards, with a big publicity assist from Capitol. The treadmill routine was also satirized in an episode of "The Simpsons."

In 2008, I spoke with Kulash, who also plays guitar in the band; his sister, Trish Sie, does the band's choreography. (Kulash is second from right in the photo.)

★ ★ ★ ★ ★

I grew up in Washinton, DC. I was a disciple of Fugazi and punk rock. Ian MacKaye from Fugazi loaned me money to put out our records in high school, and I'd go to his house to write him checks to pay him back. He was my mega-hero. Winding up on a major label ten years later seems like a strange metamorphosis.

I think if artists are making things for the right reasons, they don't really care that much for the intermediaries and distributors and middlemen. It's much nicer to have direct communication with the people you're making things for. But it puts you in the position of having to be your own business team.

The decline of the industrial media machine. Much more of this promotional stuff used to be handled by an industrial media machine of some kind. And little of it is now. It's a blessing and a curse. I think it's much more of a blessing, though. We don't have to be filtered through a whole bunch of corporate facades.

On the other hand, I really don't like self-promotion that much. I'd much rather be playing or writing.

I think the most successful things we've done, in terms of Machiavellian marketing online, had no real marketing impetus to begin with. They were just things we though would be fun to do.

The Internet is a low-risk medium. You can make a video for $5 or $5000, and if it's not super-successful, you don't have a major label breathing down your neck. You haven't wasted someone's money.

YouTube releases. Our top video on YouTube, "Here It Goes Again," has been seen 43 million times. I don't know what 43 million people look like. But I do know that when we went to Taiwan recently and played a show to 8,000 people, in a place where our record was never really pressed or promoted, we were the headliners. In Korea, we opened for the Chemical Brothers, and thousands of people knew every word to every song.

I have some theories about why our YouTube videos took off. Part of it is the homemade-ness of it. People really can just recognize when something is honest.

We'd sold 500,000 records and had a big enough fan base. We'd toured for years and years. So the videos had a little bit of a kick-start. But they were also very clearly homemade. They didn't bear all the stamps of this kind of top-down marketing push. They were eventually shown on MTV, though.

Our back yard dance video, "A Million Ways," was really a mistake. The idea was to do this dance routine at live shows, so we could break the normal expectations of a rock show, where you feel like you're doing the same thing over and over again.

We started sending it out to friends and a couple fans. It was never intended as a real video. It trickled out, and then it just took off. [The video has been seen more than two million times on YouTube.]

Then, we made the treadmill one. We waited six or nine months to put it out. We thought it was too much like the first one. But then we said, "We can't just let this thing rot. Let's just put it out."

Neither of those two songs were intended to be singles. We didn't ask the label for permission to make the videos.

> "People started doing their own versions of the treadmill routine. Today, there are many more OK Go videos out there than we could've ever produced."

In neither case did we think, "A-ha, this will get people to buy our records." It has always been our position that the reason you wind up in a rock band is you want to make stuff. You want to do creative things for a living.

Fans respond. All of a sudden, we had fans sending us videotapes and DVDs of themselves doing the dance from "A Million Ways" at a wedding or a talent show. It was so thrilling to us that we started posting them, and inviting more of them. We basically followed the lead of a good idea that seemed to emerge, and turned it into a contest. The winners got an all-expenses-paid trip to one of our shows, and they got to dance on stage with us.

People also started doing their own versions of the treadmill routine. Today, there are many more OK Go videos out there than we could've ever produced.

We also made three traditional music videos for that same album. One was shot by Olivier Gondry, Michel's brother. We got budgets from the label. One got a few spins on MTV, and they all got played a little bit in Europe. The last one we made came out after the treadmill video, for "Do What You Want," and that one stood to do pretty well through traditional channels. But then our label fired their president that same week, and everybody we knew who worked at Capitol got fired.

If making money is your aim, you need to get played on the radio. That's still where hits are made. And it's very hard for rock bands to get off the ground without tour support and promotional support from a label. If magnitude is your aim, you still have to play with all the big players.

But I also believe that in the digital age, you can be a totally obscure and difficult math rock band. But as long as your 1,500 fans are so into you that they'll support you, that's OK – that can work.

Blogs, NPR and videogames. A month after someone has written about your music on an influential blog, someone will mention it to you, and you realize that you're now big in Spain, because of this blog you never knew about.

At shows, I hear much more from kids that they first heard our music in a video game – we've been in six or ten videogames. We toured with [the NPR radio show] "This American Life" for a while, and that's such a dedicated audience. Years later, those shows are rebroadcast, and they're also available online. I've also written some op-ed pieces for the New York *Times*. I don't know if that sells albums or song downloads, of course.

Our business plan and our artistic plan have never relied on selling a lot of records. I don't actually count record sales or downloads, because we generally don't see that money anyway. But it all creates this aggregate excitement about you that's very palpable. Then, when someone asks to use your song in a movie, you can ask for three times as much, and they'll say yes.

Do we think about self-releasing our music? That's the billion-dollar question right now. We're bound by a contract to our label, and it wouldn't be worth the lawsuits. But we do think about it.

The way we have always looked at the major label structure is essentially as a bank. They take a high percentage of your revenue stream later on, but up front they'll give you tour support for a few years, and sometimes a giant advance so you can pay your bills and afford not to have a day job.

Label relations. With our label, we knew we were getting in bed with a big corporation. Some things about that suck, and some things are good. You have to guard against the bad stuff and try to magnify the good stuff.

You're always better off if you go in with your eyes wide open. Bands who think they've made it when they get a record deal have always been wrong. It's a hard place to get to, but that's really just where everything starts.

The only way you will ever be able to achieve your goals is by making the things you want to make. We've done countless collaborations, made covers of other peoples' songs, directed our own videos. It's all part of the fun project of making stuff.

In 2006, we put out an EP with the trombone band Bonerama, with me singing on it. There were a few OK Go songs and some covers. The proceeds went to musicians relief efforts in New Orleans, after Hurricane Katrina. We recorded it on our own dime, and asked the label if we could put it out ourselves. They were fine with that, but late in the game, someone in their business affairs department decided that everything that went on iTunes should really come through them. That was after we'd already set it up through iTunes.

We have a page on MySpace and a stream of photos on Flickr. The design of our Web site as it is now was paid for by the label. But we oversaw the design, and worked with the designer.

The e-mail connection. When we first started out, I wrote our e-mail newsletters, and they came from my personal e-mail account. I'd e-mail anyone who wrote back. I do a lot less e-mailing with fans these days. But I love talking to fans at shows, and I do e-mail with fans when there's a subject other than, "Oh my god I can't believe we're e-mailing with each other!" That makes me feel really self-conscious. I sometimes read the message boards on the OK Go site. My mom reads them more, though, and she sends some of the messages to me.

But it does feel like there's a very active community on our site, and I do feel like we're a part of it. Still, there's something weird and self-satisfied about jumping into the fray.

We haven't podcast in a while, but while we were touring, we made six or so. It was just us interviewing people, like our choreographer, Trish Sie, or the radio host Jonathan Goldstein. Whether they brought us any new fans, I don't know, but they were fun to make.

Five years ago, I thought that e-mail would be the main component of our relationship with our fans. But then with social sites like MySpace and Facebook, that kind of newsletter format feels a little antiquated and rigid now. People are just used to being in an environment where there's some participatory element.

We do maintain a separate e-mail list from the label. We collect them at our shows, and we share them with the label. There are a few hundred thousand people on it. If we went independent, though, I don't imagine that our e-mail list would be selling us a bajillion records.

> "Everybody's in this same Wild West environment. There are no rules."

Who else does a good job with their online stuff? Gnarls Barkley does an amazing job, striking a tone that's very well-suited to the new world. I've always been impressed with Arcade Fire online, and Of Montreal.

Could a band do it again, what we did with the YouTube videos? I don't think that you can have a revolution twice. I think that the shock of a homemade video just sweeping the world like that couldn't be replicated. And there are so many people trying to replicate it that you're just lost in a sea of all the attempts.

At the end of the day, people are interested because of the music. People who feel like some sort of distribution strategy is the answer - like, "I'm only going to distribute by peer-to-peer" - are missing that point.

But something new is always happening. The people best poised to take advantage of that are those who have a good idea in the first place, and are adventurous enough to just try to make something of it. I don't know what the next phase of the digital revolution is, but there will be another shocking moment in music distribution, or a pop culture idea.

Everybody's in the same Wild West environment. There are no rules. Anything could work.

DJ Spooky
Composer, Writer and Multimedia Artist

Where inspiration leads, DJ Spooky follows, from albums to books to movies to art installations. He has collaborated with Chuck D and Yoko Ono, had work exhibited at the Whitney Biennial and the Andy Warhol Museum, and been published by MIT Press. When we spoke in July 2008, he told me that most of his income was coming from lectures, followed by his recordings.

★ ★ ★ ★ ★

I've been on Geffen/Outpost, on independent labels, and mid-sized labels. I never really trust record labels to have their shit together. The record labels are like dinosaurs. The ball is definitely in the court of the independent artist right now.

I made an album called "Songs of a Dead Dreamer" in 1996, and that got me the attention of Geffen/Outpost. But for them, I was one amongst a zillion people, and then the label got bought. They fired all the people we'd been dealing with.

In the last several years, I've decided it's economically viable to be an independent artist. You can be more nimble.

On MySpace, I have about 15,000 friends, and I have a mailing list of about 15,000 people.

Every show I do, people sign up for the mailing list. Bill Clinton considered his presidency a permanent campaign, and that's the way you have you look at your career.

Getting an assist. I have two assistants, one who focuses on my Web site and one for MySpace. Both are very web literate. [And both are paid.] We have a rolling consensus of what the Web site should say – is this the proper thing to send to the mailing list, to have on the homepage?

I send out a message once or twice every couple of weeks. Some younger DJs send out crazy amounts of e-mail. I find myself unsubscribing.

I spent six weeks in Angola recently, and I put up a free mix of hip hop from all over Africa on my site. The blog Boing Boing linked to me, and that got a lot of buzz. It was like a link avalanche, there was so much traffic.

Free vs. paid. You give away a certain amount of your stuff, and then the cultural economy of cool kicks in. People put your tracks on their playlists, they put them in Rhapsody and Yahoo Music. From our generation's perspective, giving your work away for free is like a loss-leader.

I just published a book called *Sound Unbound,* which is about digital music and culture, and I've been really focused on my film projects, like *Rebirth of a Nation* and *Terra Nova,* which was shot in Antarctica. The book is like a calling card for lectures, and I take the film around and accompany it. I get great money for speaking and appearances, and it's an audience that usually buys the book or the DVD, too.

> "You give away a certain amount of your stuff, and then the cultural economy of cool kicks in."

Steve Cohen of Music + Art Management is my manager. Half the battle is being organized. There's a tremendous amount of stuff coming in, and you have to make sure that you get back to people quickly. I wanted to make sure that there are people who're responsible in my office. One time, somebody didn't get back to a producer who was working on a soundtrack, and we lost that opportunity. Time is everything in this Web-based culture.

I get hundreds of e-mails a day, just from fans. I try to get into a regimen of answering them over about two hours in the morning.

Managing your time. I'm usually an early adopter, but my motto for most things is that there's only 24 hours in the day. You can't expect that you're going to be able to keep up with everything. You have to give yourself some room to breathe and room to live. Maybe I'm procrastinating about Facebook, but I just think it'd be one more thing to deal with. I'm kind of a workaholic – I'm not lazy. But you have to give yourself some room to be creative, and that requires that you get a recharge someplace, sometime.

"We're seeing this intense democratization of creativity."

As an independent artist, you know that today there's an ocean of people doing releases, putting out weird MP3s. There are oceans of people making videos on YouTube. I celebrate that and enjoy that we're seeing this intense democratization of creativity.

[Note: In late 2008, DJ Spooky eventually set up a Facebook page, stocking it with photos, videos, and a discography.]

Jill Sobule
Singer-Songwriter

Jill Sobule's music has been heard nearly everywhere: from NPR to Nickelodeon, from the Huffington Post to the soundtrack of the movie "Clueless." The radio hit that launched her career, in 1995, was "I Kissed a Girl" (Fabio starred in the music video.) For fifteen years, she recorded on four different record labels, two of which went out of business. Lately, she has been experimenting with releasing live shows for free on her Web site; collaborating with Don Was to release videos on the ad-supported Web site MyDamnChannel.com; writing a soundtrack for the online comic book "Prozak and the Platypus"; and raising almost $90,000 from fans to fund her 2009 release, *California Years*.

★ ★ ★ ★ ★

Even if the old system hadn't been antiquated or fading, it hadn't been good for me. You'd try to get a record deal, get it, put out a record, and go on tour. You'd hope the record does well, and then you go through the whole cycle again.

For me, the thought of doing it again the old way felt pointless, like I'd be hitting my head against the wall. I wanted to try to figure out a new way of doing things, and not having to use my personal funds. I was lucky to have a small but mighty fan base. I feel like a mini-pioneer.

Record label relations. My first album was on MCA, their Geffen Records label. I did a second record for them. Half of it was produced by Joe Jackson, and half by Wendy and Lisa. But I got dropped by the label, and it never came out.

It was devastating. I have no marketable skills to do anything else. I quit for a little while.

But then I started writing again and playing. It's the most awful thing in the world to go into a label and play things for them. I remember going into one label, and the guy said, "I love your music. But save your deeper lyrics for a book of poetry. And also, you're not the youngest." I was, like, thirty at the time. That just devastated me.

> "I have no marketable skills to do anything else."

I did get signed by Atlantic Records two months later. They put out my second album, and I happened to see that executive again. He said, "Congratulations," since I'd just had a semi-hit with "I Kissed a Girl," and I just ripped into him. It was the best feeling. I said, in a granny voice, "Now, who are you again?"

Then I was on Beyond Records. My label-mates were Motley Crue and Sammy Hagar. Then that went under.

Then I was on Artemis Records, where Danny Goldberg [who has worked with Nirvana, Bonny Raitt, and the Beastie Boys] signed me. It went under.

I had a manager who was old-school. "Why don't you go with another label?" He was set in his ways. So I parted ways with him, and started tryng to figure out how to do all this by myself, with a different approach to recording, marketing, and distribution.

I vetted managers to try to find someone who would help me with my vision, and I found someone who I really liked.

I realized that, like a lot of artists, I was ignorant about how things are done. Trying to do everything a label does is fantastic, but it's a lot of work.

Everyone seems to have a scheme – some sort of marketing company or digital download company – and a lot of it sounds kind of gobbledy-gook to me.

My stalkers work for me now. I have a fan who builds my Web sites. I make the joke, "I make my stalkers work for me now." They stop being obsessed with you, because you're haranguing them to get things done. They're like, "Go away, Jill." Seriously, Tony Camas is a fan and a friend who has been a road manager and who handles my Web sites ever since he told me how my site wasn't so great. I do a blog there, and there's an e-mail list, and I have a profile on MySpace. Another fan is like my archivist, keeping track of wherever I show up, and when people write about me.

I have a monthly column I write in *Performing Songwriter* magazine. I've blogged on HuffingtonPost.com, and done stuff with National Public Radio. They had a morning show called "Bryant Park," and for about a year I would go on it whenever I was in New York. They'd say, "We need a song about Halloween," and I'd write one.

Crowdfunding. Originally, to fund the new album [*California Years*], my idea was for everyone to be a stockholder, have it really be the peoples' record company, whether they gave $10 or $1,000. But my lawyer said, "Forget it." With the laws, it was just ridiculously impossible. So the next step was donors, an idea that came up a few years ago.

It was brewing when I went to a few conferences where I got a chance to talk with people outside the music industry, TED and D: All Things Digital, which the Wall Street *Journal* puts on. [At the latter conference, she opened for Microsoft CEO Steve Ballmer.] That helped me more than anything else. People there gave me the encouragement to actually try to do it. One night, I came up with a bunch of sponsorship levels, and Tony helped me put the Web site together, JillsNextRecord.com.

When I first did it, I thought it'd be my mother and maybe one or two fans donating. But I put it out there, and a guy from the Associated Press picked it up, so it got on all these news sites. Then Perez Hilton put it on his gossip blog, right underneath something about Lindsay Lohan. It had my picture and a dollar sign. Even though he was being nasty, it really helped me a lot.

Then I was on a couple panels about creative financing at different conferences, and that got me a lot of interview requests.

I picked $75,000 as a fundraising goal. It was kind of off-the-cuff. Making a record can cost anywhere from $1,000 to $1,000,000. I figured I'd use the money for recording, distribution, publicity – everything.

The contribution levels went from $10, which got you a digital download of the record, to $10,000, which gave you the chance to sing on the record. A woman named Jo Pottinger from the UK donated at that level. I bought her a plane ticket, put her up at a fancy hotel for a couple nights, and I gave her a vocal lesson. She sang on the record, and a friend of mine videotaped it. She was fantastic.

I've also done a couple house concerts for people who donated $5,000, and I have one more to do, in Texas. If you donated $1,000, I said I'd write you a theme song for your answering machine, and I still have to record a few more of those.

It took me about two months to get to my $75,000 goal. [The final amount raised was close to $90,000.]

For this album, I asked everyone to pick their six favorite songs to winnow things down from 16 songs to 14. Even if it's a new world, and I could put out as many songs as I wanted, I still wanted to feel like it was an album, to have a certain flow and narrative.

I got Henry Diltz, who shot Jackson Browne and CSNY, to do some photos for the album. His best friend is a fan of mine. He has this great, early 1970s look.

Hopefully, *California Years* will be successful enough that I can fund the next one myself. Yet, I'd still want to keep the participation from the fan base in there.

I do want to just continue to keep giving my audience songs, rather than make them wait for one big album every couple of years. In the past, I've just put up songs for free on my site, but at some point, I have to figure out how to monetize it.

I still mostly make my living from live shows.

At my concerts, I'd sell these little USB key drives for $5. In two weeks, when they plugged in the key drive, it'd take them to a special Web site where they could download the recording of that show. That company is called QiGo. I see doing more of that in the future.

In the old days, you had to sell 100,000 copies of your album to matter. And with my records, I've never seen a penny from them. I got an advance, but that was it. Now, you can imagine selling 5,000 records, and still making some sort of profit. If you have a nice group of fans, they can support you.

It does help to find other ways to get your music out, whether it's in ads or movies or TV shows or radio shows.

> "It does help to find other ways to get your music out, whether it's in ads or movies or TV shows or radio shows."

Artist empowerment. Not to be cliché, but there is something really empowering about this – having your own schedule, your own timing. The record is coming out in April 2009. And if I wanted to put out a digital-only release next week, with songs about Karl Rove, and Condi, and Bush, I could do that. But I don't think I have the energy for that.

There definitely has been a benefit, for me, to having gathered a few fans the old way, through labels and their publicity efforts. But lots of people have discovered me through other things I've done independently, like songs I've published on HuffingtonPost.com, or some goofy Christmas song I've written.

On [the radio station] KROC in Los Angeles, they had me on their morning show to talk about how I raised money for the new album. I said, "I had to do it this way, because you guys aren't playing me. I just don't have the $500,000 to pay you so I get played." I don't know if they found that so funny.

Richard Cheese
Singer and Frontman, Lounge Against the Machine

The toughest interview subject to pin down for this book was new-school lounge lizard Richard Cheese, the LA-based performer famous for his cheeky covers of songs like "Gin and Juice" and "Hot for Teacher." Cheese (Mark Jonathan Davis, in real life) ducked a few of our scheduled interviews, and then when we finally connected by phone he explained that he was sure I'd misquote him. After more negotiations, he agreed to conduct the interview by e-mail.

Cheese fronts the band Lounge Against the Machine, which frequently gigs in Las Vegas. He has put out eight albums, most recently the live recording "Viva La Vodka," and has appeared on "Jimmy Kimmel Live," NBC's "Las Vegas" series, and as the house band on NBC's "Last Call with Carson Daly."

★ ★ ★ ★ ★

Scott Kirsner: Could you talk a bit about how you've built your "fan database" of e-mail addresses? Do you collect them at shows, on your Web site, or through other means?

Richard Cheese: I've got several different methods of gathering e-mail addresses:

1. I retain the e-mail address of every customer who buys something through richardcheese.com, whether it be CDs, tickets to our shows, or membership in our fan club.

2. Whenever we do a concert at a venue that sells tickets online, we ask the venue to send the ticket buyers' e-mail addresses to us, and we send them a 'thank you' e-mail and invite them to join our list.

3. We have e-mail sign-up sheets at our shows.

4. We have a sign-up link at our Web site, where visitors can add their names to our e-mail list in a form.

5. Of course, anytime someone e-mails me, we invite them to join our e-mail list, too.

SK: Do you post your own videos to YouTube, or do fans and others do that? How does it benefit you to have videos with 50,000 or 100,000 or 300,000 views there?

RC: Honestly, I tried in earnest to use YouTube as a promotional device, but because our songs are covers, there were evidently copyright restrictions, so many of the videos I posted were pulled down by YouTube. Now, any videos you might find of my songs on YouTube have been posted by fans. It has been fascinating, surprising, and probably a windfall to have these home-made videos posted and watched. To see strangers lip-synching to my songs is very surreal! In general, I'm sure YouTube helps with exposure, but I can't really tell if it's translating into CD sales.

SK: How do you use MySpace and Facebook? Have you done anything specific to promote your pages there? How do you think about the "friends" on those sites – is it easy/hard to get them to buy albums or come to shows?

RC: MySpace and Facebook have been significant parts of my marketing efforts. On MySpace, I use the bulletins feature, and I also post occasional blogs. It seems like I got a lot of traffic from MySpace fans, especially because people were posting my songs on their profiles, spreading the word. Although I have more than 60,000 friends now, it seems to have died down a bit. I think the users have become more savvy and aren't reading the bulletins as much. And there are...built-in player apps which supersede the need to visit my page's player.

Facebook is my preferred site nowadays. In just seven months, I've attracted 10,000 fans to my Richard Cheese page, and it's great that you don't have to manually approve them [as you do on MySpace]. The "Send Update To Fans" feature allows me to send them notices which they are more likely to see. Obviously, [Facebook's] targeted updates and ads are very convenient, too. When we do a show in a particular city, I'll create an ad campaign that targets that market, plus the surrounding states. Facebook seems to be very effective, and the interface is a lot easier to use.

SK: When you've been featured in newspapers or magazines or TV shows, like Jimmy Kimmel, how much does that help your career? Does it just build your rep, or does it impact sales and people showing up at your concerts? How effective do you feel it is, relative to online promotion?

RC: The use of our song ["Down with the Sickness"] in the 2004 movie *Dawn Of The Dead* is mentioned most frequently as the reason people discovered us. That movie runs on cable and people watch the DVDs, and that has been the #1 Richard Cheese viral marketing tool.

I used to think that being on a TV show would generate lots of customers, but I think the TV viewership pie is sliced so small that it's no longer an effective platform. We appeared on NBC's "Last Call with Carson Daly"

> "I used to think that being on a TV show would generate lots of customers..."

twenty times, but I don't think it had much of an impact on sales. A lot of people saw us on CNN on New Year's Eve 2007 with Anderson Cooper, but we were only on for thirty seconds, [so] I doubt anyone rushed out to buy our CD. Being on a TV show looks good on our resume, and it's nice to have the footage to use promotionally, and it's certainly fun, but unless we get a chance to perform a full song on the Grammy Awards or "Grey's Anatomy," we won't get seen by a lot of people.

Our primary hope nowadays is word-of-mouth. That's why I send out e-mail blasts, hoping that people will forward our messages to their friends.

SK: How much do you interact with fans, via e-mail/Facebook/MySpace, etc.?

RC: I honestly read every single e-mail and MySpace message personally, and I usually respond personally. If someone asks an obvious question, I send them a generic form letter to refer them to my Web site's FAQ section. But if it's a heartfelt message, I reply. I always reply to our troops serving in the military. I also have discussion boards on my Facebook page, which I try to moderate a few times a month.

SK: Can you talk about all the different products you sell online? I'm guessing the CDs generate the most income for you, but is there anything else that's really significant in terms of sales? T-shirts, thongs, autographs?

RC: Actually, CDs don't make us very much money. Because our songs are covers, we pay a substantial portion of sales to publisher royalties. We make the most profit from t-shirts, thongs, tank tops, etc. And posters are the most profitable; it's just a piece of paper and ink – very low overhead. We sell our autographs for an extra $4 per item, and I think my most loyal fans are the ones who buy them. I appreciate their support, and I personalize each autograph. We also started selling Christmas cards and greeting cards, so people can have a birthday card mailed to someone, personally signed by Richard Cheese.

SK: Could you talk about iTunes (and any other digital outlets where you sell your music)? Do you get more money from CDs than from digital, or is it neck-and-neck? Do you push one over the other for any reason?

RC: Just a few months ago, our iTunes sales eclipsed our in-store sales. However, you can't sell an autographed download, so we are continuing to push our discs online and to retail stores. Obviously, I think the wave of the future is all-digital. But there will always be people who want a physical souvenir of their experience, so we will continue to sell physical CDs.

There is certainly a savings in manufacturing costs with downloads vs. physical CDs; if we can sell our songs without paying for album jackets and discs, that's great. But with iTunes lowering its prices to 69 cents per download, I think the profit margin is getting smaller and smaller.

I do think that my fans buy our entire albums, instead of just one song at a time. I think that our music, which is essentially a novelty act, attracts fans who are somewhat cosmopolitan in their tastes. ...I think that some of my fans actually buy both our physical CDs *and* pay to download our albums into their iPods. I know that I do that with my favorite bands. Let's hope that the true fans of our band will continue to be loyal customers like this!

Chance Hutchison
Singer-Songwriter

LA-based Chance (he goes by just the one name) communes with fans on his own Web site and also a social network on Ning for the "friends of Chance." He started his self-distribution career by releasing a string of original singles, treating each one like an album unto itself – with cover art, a lyric sheet, the low-down on what inspired the song, and a "geeked out" description of how it was recorded. Though Chance is still working a day job, he plays frequently with his band The Choir around California.

★ ★ ★ ★ ★

Scott Kirsner: You had an earlier career where you worked with a label, right?

Chance: I was in a band called Portable. We had a few albums out on a very big indie label, in the late 1990s and early 2000s. I really didn't think that I could have the wool pulled over my eyes, and I did.

The label is always in control. You can't fight them unless you have bargaining power. If you're a brand-new band, and you say, "Put us on the road," they can say, "Sure, but we want you to open up for really big bands." I felt, just put me out on the road and let me slog it out. I can show my worth.

The upside was the opportunity of their built-in networks. But the label is always playing roulette. If another band seems like it's starting to take off, they move all their chips to that band, and then they move them somewhere else. It's a constant, never-ending battle to feel like you're being paid attention to. It was extremely frustrating as an artist and a business person.

SK: So how did your solo career take off?

Chance: I decided I was going to record myself, and learn the engineering side of things. It was a slow process. I released singles, starting in 2004, rather than releasing CDs. It was basically just one MP3 at a time, but I'd create a mini-event, with poster art. I did the art myself – I'm self-taught. I'd go into great detail on my site about how and why I wrote the song. I had a "geek-out" section that would talk about the gear I used. Then, once I had five singles, I'd put out a volume. I did three of those. Every single was a marketing tool, and it provided me with a chance to interact with my fans.

I had a message board on my site, and a MySpace page. On the message board, everyone would chit-chat, and I'd jump in. I wanted them to feel more of a connection to me, to break down the wall between fan and artist.

SK: Let's talk about CDs versus digital distribution.

Chance: I'd sell the CDs at shows, and on CD Baby, which gets you on iTunes. iTunes is great because it's a consistent stream of revenue. But selling it through my own site, with my online shopping cart, and at shows has been the better source of profits. Merchandise sales, like t-shirts, are pretty good, too.

People still buy CDs. Either the older fans tend to have the desire to buy the music on a physical CD, and they have the money, or the younger fans don't have the money or they're so used to getting it for free, because of piracy. At shows, it's a no-brainer: people buy the CD.

SK: Are you still working a day job?

Chance: I do have a day job. I work for Playboy TV, and I do Web sites on the side.

SK: Your music has been played a lot by podcasters, including Brian Ibbott from "Coverville," right?

Chance: My music has been on tons of podcasts. A podcaster named Jason Evangelho found me on the indie music site GarageBand.com, where I had a song that was #2 for a year on alternative rock chart, "Say

What You Will." Jason was the first podcaster who every played me on the Internet, on Insomnia Radio. Then C.C. Chapman from Accident Hash found me, and then it just snowballed. One day, a guy from Qatar e-mailed me to say, "Just so you know, your song is #2 on my radio station in Qatar, and it's going to be #1 soon." He was running the only alternative radio station in Qatar.

SK: You seem to offer your fans a lot of opportunities to get involved, to help direct what you do.

Chance: On my "Friends of Chance" message board, I let people pick a song they wanted me to cover. They could put up anything they wanted. I narrowed it down to four, and then put a poll up to let me vote on which one I should do. I did "Creep" by Radiohead, then "When Doves Cry" by Prince. Then I said, "Pick the worst song you can think of, and I'll try to make it better." They had Britney Spears, and Olivia Newton-John, and finally they picked "Milkshake," by Kelis. I was scared, because I had no idea how I was going to make it good.

> "On my message board, I let people pick a song they wanted me to cover. ...Then I said, 'Pick the worst song you can think of, and I'll try to make it better.'"

On my upcoming record, *Famous Words & Alibis*, there's a song called "You." I had this idea that the whole song would sound like a church singing a hymn together, where some are in tune and some are not. I got about thirty people to sing on it. I don't sing until the third verse. A few of them were in LA, and I had them over to my place to record. But some had access to their own studios, so they'd either mail me a disc or send me MP3s. I put a section online to explain how to do that, and gave them the stem tracks.

I'm from Orlando, and so I have an Orlando contingent of fans. For three years in a row, when I come home for Christmas, we do "Pizza with Chance." Fifteen or twenty Orlando fans meet me at this one pizza joint, and we hang out, usually right before a show.

SK: What else have you done online that has been an experiment, and what seems to work best?

Chance: I'm Twittering now. I have pages on MySpace and Facebook, and I have my blog. I think there would be far fewer people at shows if I didn't have the online presence I have. But people's attention span on the Internet is about five seconds. You have to keep that in mind.

I was doing a show in Rancho Cucamonga, and I went on this online show called High Desert Community. It's like public access television, but online. This girl Stef has a show called "Ear Candy." They've got a chat box, so you can talk to the person who's on with her. I found it riveting. The next day, I had ten or fifteen new MySpace adds, and a few more people at the Rancho Cucamonga show.

I think more bands have to be willing to do things where you're not getting a net result immediately. Everything I'm doing is like body punches. I've done a few DIY videos on YouTube. It's just more shots on goal. That's the way I look at it. Eventually, the dam's gonna crack.

Brian Ibbott
Host, "Coverville"

The podcast "Coverville" is obsessed with cover songs. Produced three times a week since September 2004, it usually focuses on covers of a single artist's work, like Prince or Dolly Parton, though occasionally its host, Brian Ibbott, will pick up another theme, like covers of James Bond theme songs. In 2007 and 2008, Apple named "Coverville" one of the year's best podcasts. Each episode of "Coverville" reaches about 15,000 listeners, and advertising and sponsorship revenue provides a big chunk of Ibbott's annual income.

★ ★ ★ ★ ★

Scott Kirsner: How did "Coverville" get started?

Brian Ibbott: It started in September 2004, right about the time that the word "podcasting" appeared. I'd heard about what [former MTV host] Adam Curry was doing, and I started listening to his podcast. I said, "This is the new way of making a radio show."

I'd wanted to be a DJ growing up. I visualized "WKRP in Cincinnati" and thought all radio was like that. In Denver, we had some great AM stations, and I was fascinated by the DJs and all the stories about the performers. I used to wonder, "Why are there two versions of 'Hooked on a Feeling?'"

I went to the Colorado Institute of Art, and then I worked in support and documentation for a software company. In the 1990s, I worked as a wedding DJ. But it was tedious, boring work. You play the same 75 songs, often in the same order. "Love Shack" goes perfectly into "Old Time Rock & Roll." I did that for about 11 months before giving up.

With podcasting, I started thinking about a show dedicated to cover music, and I recorded that first show before I knew what I was doing. I learned as I went along. Even from the very beginning, I was doing one show every three or four days. Today, the average show gets about 15,000 downloads, and there are 11,000 subscribers to the podcast.

SK: Do you still have a day job?

BI: I do consulting for companies on stuff like documentation and program development and customer support. But "Coverville" is about half my household income. I earn about $25,000 a year from it. I feel like I'm in the one percent of podcasters making decent money.

SK: How did the audience grow over time?

BI: There have been a couple big spikes. When I was getting 30 or 40 listeners an episode, one of my listeners called up Adam Curry [who had a popular podcast called "The Daily Source Code"] and sent him an MP3 of my show, and said, "You've got to check this out." Adam Curry played the call on his show, and for the next several months, he was a big supporter of "Coverville." He'd play bits of my show on his show. Traffic went crazy.

iTunes was the second big spike, when they launched the ability to publish podcasts through iTunes. Some fans of mine at Apple put "Coverville" on the front page when they launched podcasting on iTunes.

SK: Did you put your podcast on iTunes?

BI: No, it's funny. It wasn't easy to figure out how to distribute through iTunes initially. They did it for me, without even telling me. I had a regular RSS feed for the show, and they picked that up, and put some artwork in. iTunes launched podcasts, and "Coverville" was right there.

BusinessWeek contacted me for an interview about podcasting in 2005, and their article had a huge picture of me next to a small picture of Howard Stern. But I haven't done any out-going PR. I couldn't create a press release to save my life. That's one of my shortcomings.

SK: Where does the "Coverville" revenue come from?

BI: Almost all of it comes from Audible.com's sponsorship. Advertisers were approaching me from the get-go. I had Tower Records for a while, and software called iPodderX. Now, BackBeat Media sells the ads, and takes 50 percent. I direct any interested advertisers to them.

Being an affiliate with Amazon [and referring customers to their site to buy CDs] does really well. I make probably $2,000 a year on Amazon links.

The Denver *Post* newspaper was looking for a podcaster to do their news, and so I would get up every morning, find the top stories on their site, and record them for upload by 7 AM. I pitched them a few other podcast ideas, like "Today in Music History," and for a while, they were paying me $500 a week to record and produce those two podcasts. [Ibbott still does a podcast for the *Post* called "Lyrics Undercover," which explores the lyrics of popular songs.]

SK: What's your relationship with listeners like?

BI: I spend more time interacting with the audience than I spend recording and producing the show. I get 40 or 50 e-mails a day with requests, ideas, comments, and suggestions. I respond to each one, even if it's just, "Yeah, that's a great track – I'll get it in the show." I also read all the comments on the blog. I also have a forum on the site, and I see all the new messages in the forum. But the people there do a good job of managing themselves as a community. They answer each others' questions.

I'd say only about ten percent of the music on the show is stuff that I knew about. Ninety percent is recommendations from fans. Listeners are doing a great job of introducing me to stuff I wouldn't discover otherwise.

There's also a map I did on the Web site, the "Citizens of 'Coverville'" map, which lets listeners add a photo of themselves to a map, and a little comment. Then you can see where all the listeners are. [Ibbott used a free service called Frappr.] That came as a recommendation from a listener.

I fostered this community feel to the show by listening to people's suggestions, and I think they appreciate that. The person who suggests something, whether it's a song I should play or a feature for the Web site, will probably tell other people about the show. And I'm trying to generate as much word-of-mouth as possible.

Natasha Wescoat
Painter, Designer and Illustrator

Michigan-based painter and illustrator Natasha Wescoat took the leap in 2004, launching a full-time career as an artist. She sells her work on eBay, Art.com, and Etsy, and produces original artwork on commission. Her "studio cam" offers fans a live window into her work process, and her e-mail newsletter, targeted to collectors of her work, gives subscribers advance notice when new work is going up for sale. In 2007, Art Business News named her an "Emerging Artist and Trendsetter."

★ ★ ★ ★ ★

In 2004, I was 23 years old. I had two kids. Financial constraints were making things really difficult. I was in the middle of getting a degree at Delta College, a community college here in Michigan.

I'd seen other artists selling their work with eBay auctions, and I began listing some of my really large, massive abstract paintings there. It became this money-making venue for me, and then I began my own Web site.

I'd attempted to do the gallery thing, and sell in the offline world. The shows just didn't draw people, and I wasn't making as much as I could online. I got on all the message boards and started networking. I became part of these different online artists groups. I got involved in the communities, and learned from others how to market.

I started to sell stuff through Art.com. [Art.com has a program called Artist Rising, which sells prints and original art.] They had a great program for artists who wanted to make royalties from their prints.

A stylistic shift. Things really started to take off when my style changed. I got into contemporary landscapes and more whimsical pieces.

I tried doing live Webcasts, using Justin.tv. I'd have my live webcam on while I was painting. A bunch of my fans got on there to watch me paint, and they'd ask me questions through the chat window. I'd talk to them. I started auctioning small pieces that I'd make in a half-hour, and would sell them for $200 or $300. I just thought it'd be fun to try something like that, where someone could watch me make a piece and then purchase it.

What I find is that people really love being able to be in contact with you personally. Before, there was this distance between the artist and the fan. With the Internet, it's like they're your best friend. You can talk to them a million different ways. I have an e-mail newsletter, and a blog, and I also use Twitter.

> "Before, there was this distance between the artist and the fan. With the Internet, it's like they're your best friend."

I try to keep my e-mail sessions down to two a day. I get a lot of e-mails from students around the world doing reports on my work, or other artists, or fans who want to say how much my art has changed their lives. I'd tried to keep one day a week where I'd just answer e-mails, but now I'm better at doing it twice a day.

I only have about 500 people on my e-mail list. A lot of people prefer to follow the blog. Mainly, my buyers are on the e-mail list, watching for when new work is listed. People on the list find out about new work first, and I'll give them discounts and free shipping. I'm a little more personal on my e-mail list than my blog. The list is for people who are truly interested in my work, and want to watch my career.

It doesn't matter how many ways I broadcast my message. People are kind of lazy. You have to repeat yourself a lot. I'll mention something on my blog, and Twitter, and the e-mail list.

I've never had an agent. I'd always represented myself. And I'd always self-published until I did a deal recently with Winn Devon, a publisher in Seattle, to sell fine art prints of my work in places like Bed, Bath & Beyond.

TV and film exposure. A producer from "Extreme Makeover: Home Edition" bought my work for their own house. Then, I worked with them to create some specific pieces for a house they worked on, in October 2006. That increased sales exponentially, and I got really busy doing commissions. I've also had some of my work in movies on the Lifetime cable channel. Some of my work is going to be in the movie *Marley & Me*. They found me and were interested in having three pieces in the movie. I did it for free, for the promotional value.

With Art.com, I was making $5,000 a month in royalties at one point. But they made too many changes to their site, and my royalties were basically gone. I haven't seen a dime yet from Winn Devon, but my stuff hasn't shown up in retail yet, either. I still do eBay auctions, which are good.

> "I do feel overwhelmed by the amount of work I do. ... You're doing all the branding, design, and promotion."

I do feel overwhelmed by the amount of work I do. There were points where I was just constantly dealing with customers, and I stopped working altogether. You're doing all the branding, design, and promotion. I've had a couple burn-outs, where basically I'd just stop creating new work.

Supporting myself took about two years. It was harrowing for those first two. Then, in 2006, everything became a lot smoother. I got consistent commissions, and the royalties from Art.com were really nice. I could support myself decently.

Tracy White
Comics Artist

Since 1996, Tracy White has been drawing the Web comic "Traced," an autobiographical series she describes as "95 percent true."

Her introspective storytelling style owes a bit to Lynda Barry, but her aesthetic, which often relies on white lines on a black background, is very much her own. White helped pioneer the genre of Web comics, and built a strong community around her work by inviting readers to post their own comments and stories on topics like that first kiss, or smoking cigarettes. When we spoke in 2008, she was immersed in a graphic novel project for Roaring Brook Press. White was posting images from the work-in-progress on Flickr.

★ ★ ★ ★ ★

In the mid-1990s, I was at school at NYU, in the Interactive Telecommunications Program there. It was the first year the Netscape browser was available. In my class, we thought the Internet was pretty amazing, that it was a really great way to reach people. And I'd just read Scott McCloud's book, *Understanding Comics*.

We made a site for teen girls, called Gurl.com, so that maybe they wouldn't feel as alone as I did, or feel that they were so strange, or whatever it was they were. We did issues of that in our spare time, and we eventually sold it.

Shared experiences. Around 1997 or 1998, I started the site and the series "Traced." The oldest comic on that site, "Getting Drunk," was on Gurl before it was on "Traced." I think getting drunk for the first time is a shared experience that a lot of people can relate to.

I really wanted to let people post their comments on each of the comics, to further extend the idea of sharing common experiences. I really want to reach people, and it's nice to hear that I've reached them, and that they have a story.

I've had day jobs, always in new media, often for teens. I worked on the Sci-Fi Channel's Web site, and I was at the Oxygen Network working on a Web site for teens. They commissioned an animated TV series that I did for them, which ran on the network. That gave me a chance to make a few shorts, with audio. But eventually they shifted their focus away from teens.

Big projects. Now, my day job is writing a graphic novel for teens, for Roaring Brook Press. I did an online comic recently for the Lower East Side Tenement Museum, a documentary Web comic called "For Real" that is about three girls who came to New York from three different countries.

"Traced" is a calling card. It brings people to me. There's a certain serendipity to it. I've done work for other comic Web sites, like Webcomics Nation and Serializer.net. With the book, I had to find an agent who got the Internet. Having the site helped to sell my work.

> "'Traced' is a calling card. It brings people to me. There's a certain serendipity to it."

Here's how I found my agent. I read *The Unauthorized Biography of Lemony Snicket*, and I said, "Whoever is the agent for Lemony will get me." I was at a dinner, and I said, "If I could just find out who that agent is..." And someone at the dinner said, "Oh, that's my agent."

Charlotte Sheedy is the agent. She said to me that it wasn't enough to have the Web site, that I had to write and draw the entire book I wanted to do, so I did that on the side. I'd never drawn a book. It took a year. Then we shopped it around. It got bought by an editor at Penguin Books [who later moved to Roaring Brook Press.] I don't think people would've looked at the book, and I wouldn't have known that I had to draw the book, if not for Charlotte. She's working for me by introducing my work to people.

Online, I can represent myself.

The business model. There isn't a devious business model here. There should be. I'm woefully far behind in terms of making t-shirts, and I think a lot of the income people doing Web comics today are generating is coming from t-shirts. They're really popular.

When I go to comic conventions, I sell t-shirts, and I give away coasters that say "Getting Drunk," with a picture of a girl puking in a toilet. Giving away things for free is a good way to get your name out there, and the coasters are cheap if you buy a few thousand of them. At these conventions, you reach a lot of people who wouldn't ordinarily come to your site. I go to Comic-con and the Alternative Press Expo and SPX [Small Press Expo] in Bethesda. In 2002, I was nominated for Best Online Comic at SPX, and that definitely got me a lot of exposure. I've been on a lot of panels, and in a documentary about Web comics, and some books – just because I've been around for a while.

I e-mailed Scott McCloud early on, and he became a friend and mentor. I've met a lot of people through him. And he lists me on his site, so a lot of people find me through that.

I still teach at NYU, in the Interactive Telecommunications Program. It's a class on storytelling, comics, and interactivity.

I guess my most devious business model is giving things away for free, have people come to me, and see what comes up. I usually do one or two really big projects a year.

Matt W. Moore
Artist and Graphic Designer

Matt W. Moore is an artist and designer based in Portland, Maine, who has designed car ads, fonts, logos, skateboards, wallpaper, and magazine spreads for clients like *Entertainment Weekly* and *Wired.* (He also designed the cover of this book.) He dubs his colorful, high-energy style "vectorfunk," and has had his work shown in art galleries from London to Tokyo to Milan. He also self-

publishes his own print collections, calendars, posters and books, and sells them through his site. We corresponded by e-mail for this interview.

★ ★ ★ ★ ★

Scott Kirsner: Tell me about leaving your full-time gig at Burton, the snowboard and clothing company up in Vermont. What were you doing there? Were you doing freelance work on the side?

Matt W. Moore: I worked at Burton for a year as part of their in house design team called Syndicate. I was technically a Web designer, but also had the opportunity to do identity work, participate in print and catalog efforts, sit in on strategy meetings, and even design a set of 09 snowboards. It was a great experience, a great talented bunch! During this time, my side-hustle as MWM Graphics was gaining momentum and I was working on a range of projects, from print ads for automobiles to gallery shows to logos... pretty much anything that was not in violation of my "SSS (Skate. Snow. Surf.) Non-Compete Agreement."

SK: What made you believe that you could make a living on your own?

MWM: I always had faith that I could do it on my own, if I could dedicate all of my time towards freelance endeavors. It got to the point that I was turning down freelance jobs because I physically couldn't meet deadlines as a "moonlighter." Opportunities were flowing more frequently, and with larger budgets. I decided to just go for it. Carpe diem.

SK: How do you market yourself and generate new assignments and commissions? What works best? What have you tried that hasn't really worked?

MWM: I try to do it all. Frequent Web site updates, press releases, promo books and posters, physically attend tradeshows and industry parties, street-level sticker campaigns, magazine interviews, work featured in design and illustration books, staying in touch with former clients, and reaching out to prospective clients. With the exception of sending free promos of my books, tees, and posters, my efforts are 100 percent free. The days of needing to buy a $5,000 half-page ad in a directory are long gone. A good cyber press push can reach a hundred times as many people, within 24 hours, for free.

SK: What role does your blog play in all of this?

MWM: My blog is great for many reasons. It keeps me excited and eager to share new work, it keeps me front-of-mind with fans and clients, it archives my evolution, and it serves as an all-access press releases that I upload photos and descriptions for writers and editors to reference for features. ...On a regular basis, I get a call within a couple days of posting a new design or illustration, and the client wants something just like it.

SK: How about your self-published books? Do they generate income, or are they more marketing/reputation-building pieces?

MWM: The books serve many purposes. Most importantly, they are cohesive personal efforts that become time capsules of different chapters of my art and design. ...I do sell them, and in the last couple years they have been selling out quicker. I do also send out...the books as gifts and promo pieces to key colleagues, clients, prospective clients, publishers, and taste-makers. Ultimately, my goal is to make great work, share it, sell enough to cover my investment, and add to my momentum in hopes that one day I will be able to have a massive book published with all of them in it.

SK: What's the breakdown of work that you find yourself doing lately?

MWM: It varies from day to day, and month to month, but in general my ratios are 1/4 apparel/textile design, 1/4 high-profile advertising, 1/4 identity/logos/editorials, and 1/4 personal work. I love the range of projects. It keeps me inspired and trying new things.

SK: Tell me about the stuff you sell in your online shop.... what sells best? What's the difference between stuff you publish or produce yourself, versus stuff like the wallpaper or skateboard decks, which other people make?

MWM: ...I've learned that people are much more interested in posters and prints, versus books. So the past few "books" have been released as unbound books. They are sets of high-quality prints on heavy paper, ready for frames. The collaborative projects, like the skateboards and wallpapers have been very well-received, and it is nice to have other companies handling investment, overhead, distro and hype. Doing these royalty-based collaborations is great. I would not be able to do them on my own.

SK: What advice do you have for other artists who want to make a living working independently, as you do?

MWM: The most important advice I have for any creative person is "Do you." Figure out what you love, what you are good at, what your market is, and how you are going to contribute to the future of visual culture. Self-promotion is crucial. Seriously, you must be comfortable with pitching yourself and your services. And you must do this every day, non-stop. Even if it takes five years before they start to call you back, if you were positive and genuine in your approach, prospective clients will become clients eventually. Networking is key, both in cyberspace and real life. And finally, have faith, have fun, and mind your books! Half of this hustle is definitely not "creative."

SK: I always like to ask: do you make more today than you made at any of your full-time jobs?

MWM: Yes. I make more now. :)

Dave Kellett
Comics Artist

After dreaming of a career in the funny pages, Dave Kellett discovered that the pay wasn't so great. He eventually moved his daily strip "Sheldon" entirely online, supporting the venture with a collection of books, posters, buttons, and t-shirts for sale.

"Sheldon"'s title character is a ten-year old boy who has made billions starting and selling a software company. Kellett launched the strip while in graduate school, and kept it going for several years before it became his sole source of income.

★ ★ ★ ★ ★

"Sheldon" started in 1997 or 1998, online. I was in grad school in England, and I wanted to share it with friends. It went from 25 people seeing the installments to 75 people, and then it was 500 people. You start to realize that it's spreading on its own, and you're not doing any work to make that happen.

My career goal was always to get into newspapers. For a cartoonist, that was always the mecca. In 2000, I got my strip picked up by United Media Syndicate.

Two things came out of that. One, I realized that the money in newspapers, even back in 2000 or 2001, was so small as to really kill my hopes of a newspaper career. I had this idea that everyone would be making Charles Schultz or Mort Walker money.

But I also figured out that there might be money online. Maybe not enough for a traditional business with a brick-and-mortar office and a receptionist and an executive editor, like the syndicates had, but money just the same.

Escaping the contract. I asked to be let out of my contract with United Media, and decided to go solo, around 2001. They had a terrible business model online. They'd give away the most recent thirty days of the strip, trying to entice people to buy a subscription, but the only business that has been able to make that work online is the Wall Street *Journal*.

I figured that the way to do it is to give out your complete archives for free, which increases the viral nature of the site, and it turns casual fans into die-hard fans, and even evangelists for your art online. It can take years of relationship-building before someone considers themselves a fan, and is willing to plunk down money. The United Media Web approach was the wrong approach.

Spread the strip. So in 2001, I went independent, and encouraged people to share the strip with others by e-mail, or sending electronic postcards, or taking the images and putting them wherever they wanted. Sure enough, the readership spiked noticeably.

I've never spent a dime on marketing, PR, or advertising. I found that if you make it easy for people to share the stuff, and put out good work, the very nature of the Web is such that your work will be shared. That's especially true with humor.

When I was with United Media, and a few years after that, I was working as a senior toy designer for Mattel. In January of 2006, I left that job. A year or two before that, the income was enough to leave, but I'm conservative enough that I wanted to save up two years' worth of living expenses.

Diversified income. I have three or four different income streams. One is advertising. That brings in between 10 percent and 20 percent of my income. Another is merchandise, like books and t-shirts. That's probably 40 percent of my income, while selling original art is about 20 percent. The third is speaking engagements and comics conventions, which is about 10 percent, and then I guess another 10 percent or so is miscellaneous stuff.

You need to maintain a few different income sources, so if one dries up, it's just a punch in the ribs, and not a knock-out blow. I used to use Adsdaq for advertising, and that was generating $10,000 a year at one point. But it's now drying up, and so I use three or four different ad systems.

The money involved and the quality of items produced with print-on-demand is terrible. I like to go high-quality with the t-shirts and books I produce. So I keep that all in-house. Print-on-demand is going the easy route, but I think you'll still have to have a second job.

Super-fans. Some of my fans are really kind of super-fans. They're say, "If you ship the books to me in Miami, I can bring them to the signing for you." Or they'll give you a ride to the airport in Seattle.

> "I think that those 20 percent of your fans, the super-fans, produce 80 percent of the kerfluffle around your strip."

I think that those 20 percent of your fans, the super-fans, produce 80 percent of the kerfluffle around your strip. They produce the most blog posts, they support it financially, and they go out of their way to see how they can help, both in the physical world and online.

With incoming e-mails, I try to respond to every e-mail I get, though I don't necessarily get to every blog post or forum post or Twitter message. But I think that pays itself back in terms of the bond that people feel to the artist and the strip, and eventually the books. It has a concrete business result.

There's very much a stigma on self-publishing, and I think it's going to be a little hard to shake. Virtually since Gutenberg invented the press, someone else has fronted the money to publish books. That second-party validation was a kind of seal of approval for readers. But every cartoonist I know who has a deal with Harcourt or Random House or King Features or United – they're all desperately worried about their future, and I have no worries about my future.

If I'm a new author or artist, I have to first please my editor, who has to please the publisher, who has to please the buyer for Barnes & Noble, who has to in turn entice all the readers. I bypass all those intermediary steps, and just have to entice the readers. My business is reliant on 20,000 or 30,000 bosses, rather than five bosses.

Oh, and if your editor gets fired, or your publisher goes bankrupt, or Borders goes bankrupt, you're screwed.

Selling direct. I've intentionally avoided selling through Amazon and bookstores. I already have the reader on my site. Why send them to Amazon? Why send them to a second party who will take a cut? Amazon only works when you can't reach your own audience.

From the perspective of someone who has a mortgage in LA and a new baby, I understand why people don't want to put in the time it takes to develop an audience and a business, or who don't think they can make it work. It's definitely an investment of time – maybe close to a decade – but most careers take a decade or so of investment before something really happens. Think about a doctor. The careers worth having are worth working for over years and years.

I schedule my books to come out around two big events. One is put out in late November for Christmas shopping, and the other comes out in mid-summer in time Comic-Con.

My traffic is between 1.5 million to two million page views a month. About 6,000 people read the comic by RSS, and 3,500 get it by e-mail. Every day, about 18,000 or 20,000 people read the comic on the site. It's quantitatively not that many people, yet I'm making a very comfortable living.

As an artist, you have to do it because you love it. If you're doing it for that reason first, you'll find you're producing better work, which attracts an audience. They can tell when you're enjoying it. That carries you through what are going to be lean years. There were years when the strip made only $15,000 or $20,000.

The Web is such an evolving thing. You have to ask, "What should I be doing in the future? What am I doing now that isn't working anymore?" You need to constantly be researching and writing online. How are people making money? You have to have an almost voracious appetite to follow what people are doing, and what's working, and be able to adapt and change.

Dylan Meconis
Graphic Novelist

Dylan Meconis began drawing "Bite Me," an online graphic novel about vampires, while still in high school. She's now living in Portland, drawing the online graphic novel "Family Man," about a young German scholar living during the Age of Reason, and working as a commercial artist for the design firm XPLANE.

★ ★ ★ ★ ★

I started putting my drawings and animations up in online forums when I was in high school, just to get people to look at them and get some feedback. I'd basically been writing stories and drawing pictures since I was able to. I really liked doing it, but I didn't think you could make a living doing it. I thought I would be a therapist or a teacher.

At Wesleyan, I didn't study art. I focused on literature and history.

I started my first story, "Bite Me," in high school, and did the majority of the work while I was in college. I finished in my junior year. I was doing weekly updates that whole time, and putting them on the Internet. I did one page of it a week, and I didn't script anything beforehand. I got feedback from fellow students at Wesleyan, and I'd hear from other people through e-mail. Then, people would mention my work on their blog, or in a newsletter of some kind.

Exchanging art. People would send you fan art depicting your characters, which was fun and flattering. I'd find other creators whose work I liked, and we'd do art of each others' characters, or send visual jokes back and forth. Sometimes, I'd do a doodle and put it on my LiveJournal blog, and get comments about it.

The weekly aspect of it makes you feel like you're continuously engaged in this process, as opposed to sitting a corner and working for a year. Having a steady schedule means that people know to go to your site every week. It encourages them to stick around and interact with you.

For some people, pleasing the audience can turn into a full-time job. Generally, the product isn't very good. It becomes art by the dictates of the mob.

Subscription sites. For a long time, my comic was part of a subscription-based site called Girlamatic. New pages were free, but people would pay to see the archives. It did cut down the audience a bit, but it meant that I was sort of being paid for the work. It wasn't a lot of money, but it paid my rent one month when I was unemployed, and I didn't have to pay for my own Web hosting. I think it was a good move at the time, but now it's a lot easier to be an independent artist.

Four-and-half years after I finished "Bite Me," I'm putting it in print form. I decided I didn't want to publish it through a major publisher, because I'd drawn a lot of it when I was 17. I decided I wanted to print it in a way that served people who already knew it and liked it.

Some people are amazing business managers for themselves, and some people have a life. I think that's why I still have a day job. I'm a designer at a design, illustration, and consulting firm, doing cartoons and illustrations for major corporations. Having worked freelance before, it's really nice knowing that you're going to have a paycheck twice a month. And I still feel like I'm at a point in my career where I'm being formed. It's useful to spend a few years watching how people have desgned their lives and careers, and see who's happy and who's not.

What I've sold. In terms of commerce, I've made short comics that I've sold on the Internet and in person. I've printed t-shirts, and I've sold original art. I think it's easier to sell stuff at comic shows, where you hand it to the person and they give you cash. Then you go home and buy groceries with that cash. But I've also sold stuff online.

If I suddenly lost my job tomorrow and I needed to create a self-promotional empire, I think I could do it in a month.

With "Family Man," I still try to put something up every week. That's a bit more serious – historical fiction with a twist. The audience is very involved and smart. It's neat to get feedback from people who like the historical details, or are wondering where the plot is going to go. People will correct my German. And I've told people that there are going to be werewolves, so there has been two years' worth of speculation about how this will happen.

I write notes on every installment, and people read them and can add their own knowledge on the LiveJournal site. It makes me seem smarter.

I took a year off between "Bite Me" and "Family Man," while I was finishing college and writing my senior thesis. A year off in Internet time is like a century.

I just started a podcast a few months ago. I'm doing that once every two months. I just decided that it would be fun. People can ask questions on the blog, and I answer them on the podcast.

Traffic obsession. I think if you focus too much on your traffic, that way, madness lies. I know people who check their stats every hour. I'll look every now and then, and I'll be happy if they seem high. I try not to pay too much attention to things like how many times the podcast has been listened to.

What is great about the Web is that there are no focus groups. You come by your audience honestly. They wander across you, and if they like your work, they stick around.

The commercial art I do and my Web comics are at opposite ends of the spectrum of creative control. With my comics, I get to run the entire little world.

Almost all of the big projects I've gotten have been through a social connection - something passed my way by a friend or acquaintance - or someone who visits my Web site and says, "I'm interested in having you do this." The science biography that I illustrated, *Wire Mothers: Harry Harlow and the Science of Love*, happened because Carla Speed McNeil got the offer, and recommended me to the publisher instead. I feel like everything about my life is the result of having had a Web site with a comic on it that people saw and enjoyed. My day job is a result of that... the people I live with... and the group studio that I belong to.

I think getting a scanner for Christmas, and putting up a comic on a free Web site was the most brilliant thing I did as a teenager.

Sarah Mlynowski
Novelist

Sarah Mlynowski began her writing career while working in the marketing department of Toronto-based Harlequin Books, the legendary purveyor of paperback romances. Her first novel, *Milkrun*, focused on the travails of a suddenly-single twenty-something in Boston. It was published by Red Dress Ink, a newly-created division of Harlequin. Since then, Mlynowski has published six novels for adults, and five for teens (the latter set published by a division of Random House) – and has actively experimented with new ways of connecting with her readership, from Facebook advertising to events held in the virtual realm There.com.

★ ★ ★ ★ ★

I used to work in the marketing department at Harlequin Books in Toronto. My first novel, *Milkrun*, came out in December 2001. I definitely didn't have a Web site then.

After that first book came out, I had a two-book contract for *Fishbowl* and *As Seen on TV*, and my husband was moving to New York. Everything happened at the same time. So I left my job and started writing full-time.

I think I created my Web site right before my third book came out, around 2003. I paid for it on my own. Since I'd been in marketing, I was definitely focused on how to get the word out. I put a contact page on there right away. Some writers don't like to be contacted, but I love reader mail. The form on the site goes right to my inbox. I also started asking readers for their e-mail address and where they live. Now, that's on every page of the site, but originally you had to kind of hunt for it. My Web designer puts all that info into an Excel spreadsheet, so that if I'm doing an event in a specific city, I can just e-mail the people who live in Toronto or San Francisco. I think the list is now about 7,000 people globally. I've sold most of my books overseas. If I ever do tour in Brazil, I'm ready to promote those events.

Initially, I sent out e-mail newsletters manually, doing twenty at a time. But then I joined Constant Contact, which is great for managing e-mail lists. Maybe I send out four or five newsletters a year, around a book's publication or a big event.

Colonizing MySpace. I started with MySpace and found that there weren't that many writers there. I searched MySpace to see who had listed any of my books as favorites there, and I friended them. Quickly, the friends started to add up. I have about 5,000 now. With a few other teen writers, we started a group called Teen Lit on MySpace. We put up covers of new books, and readers join because their favorite writers are involved. That group has more than 15,000 members.

These days, there seems to be less growth on MySpace, but Facebook seems to really be taking off. Most of my communications with readers are through Facebook. I joined it, and quickly discovered it was a great place to market books, because teens were really starting to flock to it. When I started, Facebook hadn't yet established fan pages. But in 2008, I started a "Magic in Manhattan" fan page for that series of my teen books.

> "These days, there seems to be less growth on MySpace, but Facebook seems to really be taking off. Most of my communications with readers are through Facebook."

Facebook ads. I've also done some advertising on Facebook. I created a little ad with the cover of my book *Spells and Sleeping Bags*. It had just been a "hot pick" in *Cosmo Girl*. The ad said, "*Spells and Sleeping Bags* is now in paperback. Visit the 'Magic in Manhattan' fan page for book info and to find the perfect spell." I targeted the ad to age 16 and younger, and to girls who said they liked Hannah Montana. I think I set a daily budget of $10, and did it for a few weeks just to see. Traffic to the fan page really went up. And whenever someone joins, the news goes out to all their friends. It says, "Julie is now a fan of 'Magic in Manhattan.'"

When people become a fan, I also friend them from my personal Facebook profile. Why? I'm ultimately looking to build my career. This series is probably going to end after four books, so I want people to be aware of the next books I write. And when they're friends with me directly, and not just the fan page, I feel like the relationship is a little more intimate.

When you are published with someone like Random House, unfortunately you can't really tell whether something like my Facebook ads has a real impact on sales. We don't have access to BookScan [which tracks week-to-week sales of individual titles], like the publishers do.

Virtual vs. in-person events. I love interacting with readers at bookstore events – talking to real people. Even if eight people show up, the store still has 100 copies of your book in stock, and they'll be pushing those copies. Plus, you get to meet the booksellers. They also do in-store displays, which are good advertising. When I'm at events and I ask girls how they knew about the event or the book, some say they saw it on my Web site or they got my e-mail, and half of them say they saw the poster in the store.

Combining those in-person events with virtual stuff is probably the ultimate. But if you're footing the bill yourself, I think online promotion can work. A four-week or six-week book tour costs a fortune.

I was doing a speech at a conference about teen girls and their fantasies. I posted on Facebook and asked my readers what their ideal fantasy is, in terms of romance – what do they want in a male hero. Do you want the best friend, or the rebel? I got twenty ideas immediately.

Relationship with Random House. I think it's a huge mistake just to hand things over to the publisher. I'm a firm believer that part of my advance should be used to promote my books. A few years ago, I hired a company to create these fun posters, and put them up in six cities, in teen clothing stores.

But they are a big help. With the Facebook fan page, I had questions, because I really didn't know code, or how to post images. So I spoke to a new media person at Random House, and she became an administrator on the fan page.

Random House also organized some events in the virtual world There.com. There were tons of fans there, all dressed up like characters from the books. We did a bunch of different events over a couple hours, in different areas of There. In each event, about 60 percent of the people were readers, but the rest were just people hanging out. I got lots of e-mail afterward from people who'd been there.

And we've worked together on things. Random House sponsors a book trailer competition, where they choose a couple of books and invite people to make book trailers. This student, Ben Cox, created an adorable book trailer for *Parties and Potions*, and I thought it would be amazing if I could put that on television. My husband had gone to school with someone who puts ads on the air in very specific markets, and so we talked about how much it would cost, and how we could do this. Random House said it was OK to use the trailer, and Ben cut it down to thirty seconds. Random House helped me focus on the right markets. We ran it in a few markets on ABC Family, for two weeks. It cost about $10,000. I thought in terms of books: if I can sell an extra 6,000 copies of the book, then it's worth it for me.

Analyzing what works. I use Google Analytics to see where the links to my Web site are coming from, what's producing the most traffic. We did a campaign recently, with Random House's support, where I did interviews on a lot of blogs. I said, "Do we also want to reach out to other teen authors, and have them ask me questions?" I have them a list of friends that I've met over the years. It turned out that I got the most traffic from those other authors' Web sites. When someone like Ally Carter, a bestselling author who has a similar audience, put me on her blog, that worked really well. And that's something that authors could do on their own, without a publisher's involvement.

Connecting to readers is so important. You can't be afraid of new technology. You have to embrace it and see if it works. If it's not working, don't waste your time. I feel like I've joined a hundred different social networks, trying to see what works. If there's a pull on the line, I stick with it. I'm still trying to figure out Twitter. I have friends who love it. But most of the teens I've spoken to aren't on Twitter.

Brunonia Barry
Novelist

Brunonia Barry and her husband, Gary Ward, spent $50,000 setting up a small press to publish Barry's first novel, *The Lace Reader*, about the investigation that follows a mysterious drowning in modern-day Salem, Massachusetts. Her first two marketing initiatives were to reach out to book groups around Salem, and to set up a Web site that would spotlight the book's reviews and help early readers spread positive word of mouth. Shortly after the book started appearing on store shelves around New England, it was optioned to  become a movie, and a division of HarperCollins signed Barry to a two-book deal for $2 million. The publisher printed 200,000 copies of the book, and it soon landed on the New York *Times* best-seller list.

★ ★ ★ ★ ★

Brunonia Barry: In the beginning, when I had only written fifty pages of the book, I sent it to two agents. It took about a year for them to write back, and they said, "We'd like to see it again when it's finished." I thought, "We can't do this." It just seemed so old-fashioned. My husband and I had our own software publishing company, focused on games, and so we naively thought that self-publishing would be the way to go. And we thought we could do a lot with the Web site.

I'd done some signings at the Spirit of '76 Bookstore in Marblehead, Mass., when I'd written a novel for the Beacon Street Girls series. That wasn't under my name. The store had 35 book clubs that they sold to regularly, and I asked them, "Could you give me one book club that might like to work with a new author?" They found a group for me, and I sent them a copy of the manuscript – really just a box of typed pages. I had them over to my house for tea, and they were very brutal. I said, "Tell me every place you stopped reading." I found it was often the same spots for everyone. So I revised it based on that.

But we knew we were going to publish it, so I asked, "Would you recommend this to other book clubs?" And they said, "We're already telling other people about it."

Gary Ward: Book groups are viral. They love to talk about what they just read.

BB: We started our own press, Flap Jacket Press, and we got a distributor, Blue Sky Media Group, to include us in their catalog. We didn't think iUniverse was the best solution. There's a certain look to print-on-demand that we didn't like, and the bookstores shied away from the look of print-on-demand, we thought. That's changing, but we wanted to do a trade paperback. We never did a hardcover. We thought with a lower price point, people would be more willing to risk that on a new book. We spent quite a bit of time and effort on typesetting and working with copyeditors – everything we thought a publisher would do.

> "Book groups are viral. They love to talk about what they just read."

We kept a list of all the people or book clubs who were interested in the book. By the time the book came out, there were 37 book clubs ready to buy it. We thought it would be a New England book, but it got to Florida and California, just by one book club talking to another book club. Anytime a new review came out, we'd send it to that e-mail list we had.

GW: I think we had the site up and running three or four months before the book was on sale. When reviewers got the book, we wanted to have an online presence. We used elements given to us by the artist who designed the book cover for us, and we hired a technical guy to put the site together.

The site had the cover of the book, sample chapters in PDF form, and all sorts of quotes from readers. We had a section called "About Salem," where the book is set. We had a guide for reading groups. The Web site was in part intended to encourage bookstores to carry the book. It was designed to be easy to navigate, with no Flash.

There was also a way to e-mail quotes from the book to a friend, like, "There's lace in every living thing." We also created electronic postcards you could send, with the cover of the book and various quotes like that.

BB: We added content regularly, so the search engines would see it changing and pick it up.

GW: We didn't actually have a link to Amazon. We wanted people to go through the independent booksellers. That was our first focus. Because we were going around trying to put physical books into the bookstores, that's where we wanted to drive people.

BB: We hired a book publicist locally, Kelley & Hall. They got the book into *Publisher's Weekly*, which gave it a great review.

Our book came out in October of 2007. We'd printed 2000 copies, and they were selling pretty well. We started to get some reorders from stores that had sold out.

The *Publisher's Weekly* review caused Hollywood agents to start to call, who wanted to do quick movie options. But that eventually got us to The Endeavor Agency. They wound up handling the movie rights. And they said, "Do you mind if we get you a bigger publisher?" So then it went to auction, and got sold at the Frankfurt Book Fair. [Barry sold *The Lace Reader* and her next book for more than $2 million, one of the richest deals ever for a self-published first novel.]

When HarperCollins bought the rights, we had to stop selling our self-published version, even though I thought we were building momentum. Their version came out in July 2008.

While I was on tour, I was lucky to do a blog entry once a week. The entries post on my site, and on Amazon, too. I can put a few lines there, about what I'm reading or doing. It doesn't have the circulation that *The Lace Reader* itself does, but I do get comments.

Lisa Genova
Novelist

Tremendously affected by the Alzheimer's disease that descended upon her grandmother, Lisa Genova channeled the experience into her first novel, *Still Alice*, about a 50-year old Harvard professor who suffers from early-onset Alzheimer's. Genova, trained as a neuroscientist, first published the novel herself. She used bookstore events, a prominent blog, a publicity firm, and her own Web site to generate awareness of it. In 2009, the book was republished by Simon & Schuster – and it debuted at #5 on the New York *Times'* fiction best-seller list.

★ ★ ★ ★ ★

Scott Kirsner: Tell me about the origins of the self-published version of *Still Alice*.

Lisa Genova: Before I self-published *Still Alice* in 2007, I was sending out the manuscript, trying to get literary agents to take it. No one did.

I also sent it to the National Alzheimer's Association, because it's about Alzheimer's disease. Their marketing rep got back to me and said they loved the book. They can't sell books on their Web site, but they said they could promote it, and recommend it as a gift. They were also launching a new campaign called "Voice, Move, Open" – a big celebrity campaign with people like Dick Van Dyke and Olympia Dukakis and Spike Lee. They asked if I would write the blog for that campaign. I did, and at the end of each entry, I included a link to StillAlice.com.

The blog was in the spring and early summer of 2007, and I self-published the book through iUniverse in July. So I had this national audience that was going to my Web site.

SK: Were you collecting people's e-mail addresses on your site?

LG: No. I wasn't collecting e-mail addresses. I built the Web site myself. I have a Mac, and I just used iWeb. I'm not that computer-savvy.

SK: What was on the site, and when did it go up?

LG: I had an excerpt, a list of events, an "about the author" page, and a "thank you page." My husband, who is a documentary filmmaker and photographer, shot some video of me, and we put that up on the site. At one point, I had an audio recording of me reading an excerpt. I just used my video camera with just audio, not video, to do that.

As soon as the book was available on iUniverse, I had a link to that site, and then I changed the link to Amazon when the book was available there.

My Web site was up before I'd even finished writing the book. I'd only written five chapters when it went up. When I finished each chapter, I'd post an excerpt. I had a few aunts and some friends who were reading it as I wrote it, and when they'd say something about it, I'd throw up a quote on the Web site. Nobody else had to know it was one of my aunts. Somehow, for me, it made it tangible. It made it feel like it was going to be a real thing.

SK: You also did a lot of old-fashioned offline promotion, right?

LG: I gave a lot of books away to people who were in the media, or people who were just loud and knew a lot of people. We got the book into local newspapers, and I was offering to do readings and signings at local indie bookstores. I tried to do two events a month. I was six months pregnant at the time, so two events was plenty. I had postcards, and I'd put them up everywhere: cafés and libraries,

SK: Were the bookstores skeptical of you, because you were self-published?

LG: Everyone was fantastic about it, except for one. There was one bookstore that just wouldn't return my e-mails or phone calls or talk to me at the store. But now, since I've been published by Simon & Schuster, they've invited me.

SK: Are you going to go?

LG: Yes, but you can bet I'll have something to say about supporting local authors.

SK: How did the economics of self-publishing work for you?

LG: I understood from Day One that as a self-published title, I would probably never make a living. I thought, "I'm never going to reach the hundreds of thousands of people I need to reach." You either make $2 a book at Amazon and $4 at iUniverse, and maybe between $2 and $4 if you sell them on consignment at bookstores. Also, I was donating $1 a book to the National Alzheimer's Association. I knew I'd be lucky to sell 1,000 on Amazon and out of the trunk of my car.

I was really only trying to sell enough to create a big-enough buzz so that the publishing industry would come around and buy it. That was always the master plan. So I didn't think, "I can't possibly give away ten of my books." It was an investment. I tried to put the book in as many people's hands as possible. I gave them to silent auctions and benefits, things like that.

SK: What else were you doing online to try to get some momentum?

LG: I was commenting on people's blogs and mentioning my Web site. I was reviewing other peoples' books on Amazon and Shelfari and mentioning my book. I was on a lot of social networking sites, like Facebook, MySpace, Goodreads, and AuthorsDen.

SK: What do you think happened that got other publishers interested in *Still Alice?*

LG: There were exactly two things that happened. In January 2008, I read an article in the Boston *Globe* about Brunonia Barry. It mentioned that she had hired Kelley & Hall Book Publicity to work with her, and that she'd gotten a $2 million advance for two books. That completely amped up the size of my dreams. I had no idea how much a book deal could go for.

At that point, enough people were liking my book who weren't directly related to me. I hired Kelley & Hall for three months, and told them that my goal was to create enough buzz to get the book picked up. In March 2008, I got on the Boston Fox TV affiliate. That weekend, there was a column about the book in the *Globe*. Kelley & Hall got the book into the hands of Beverly Beckham there, and she wrote the most fantastic column.

An author named Julia Fox Garrison, who wrote *Don't Leave Me This Way*, wrote to Beverly. She said, "Thanks for writing such a nice article about a self-published author." Julia had originally self-published her book, too, and she went on to get published by HarperCollins. Beverly forwarded the e-mail to me, and so of course I e-mailed Julia to ask if she had any advice. She introduced me to her agent.

The second thing was, my loud and large Italian family was telling everyone to buy my book. On my mom's side of the family, her cousin's husband happened to be a sales executive at Simon & Schuster. She never really thought about that, but he read the book and passed it along to someone else there. At around the same time I signed up with my agent, I got a call from them.

Pretty soon after, the book went up for auction. Three houses bid on it, and it sold to Simon & Schuster.

SK: What's it like to have them helping out with the marketing and publicity now?

LG: They fill so many roles that I had to do by myself. But at the same time, I still manage my Web site and post on my blog. When I was in Denver a few weeks ago, I did a TV segment on the morning show out there. My husband put that up on YouTube, and I embedded that into my Web site.

I've still got my e-mail address on the site. Readers can contact me directly, offer feedback, and ask if I can participate in different kinds of events. I've been getting pretty flooded. I just signed up with a speaker's bureau, run by Simon & Schuster, to handle speaking requests. I get three or four requests a day. I still Twitter, and do all my social networking sites, on my own. Simon & Schuster can't really take care of that, and if they did, it would be kind of hollow. There's a nice synergy between the more personal stuff I'm capable of doing and the bigger stuff they can do.

SK: Was there much lag-time between when they bought your book and when it came out?

LG: No. I was lucky. They bought it on the last day of May 2008, and it came out on January 6th of 2009. They ended up using cover art that came from the concept that my husband had designed for the self-published book. And I'd collected a lot of blurbs from experts and authors, and every quote that's on the back of the Simon & Schuster edition, I collected. My agent said, "This is like warp speed for the publishing industry."

I just signed a two-book deal [in February 2009] with Simon & Schuster. I did give them the right-of-first-refusal for my next book, but if we didn't like the offer, we could shop it elsewhere. They made a great offer.

I don't think I'd want to go back to self-publishing, just to see if I could go it alone. The whole point was to get into the industry.

SK: What do you think got the book onto the New York *Times'* best-seller list, in January 2009?

LG: Simon & Schuster did a lot. Getting on the list is all about sales velocity. They did a lot with sending out advance reader copies to all the Borders and Barnes & Noble stores. They sent me to some of the key trade shows. They helped get it front-of-the-store placement, and they also made sure that stores didn't put it out before the publication date.

SK: You said "yes" to this interview really quickly. Is that a sign of your willingness to do publicity in general?

LG: I say "yes" to every publicity opportunity I can, without being awful to my family. I try to schedule things for after my kids are in bed. [We spoke at 8:30 PM.] I devote about twenty hours a week to writing and to publicity, and the rest of my time is for my family.

Kris Holloway
Non-Fiction Author

Kris Holloway's first book, *Monique and the Mango Rains*, tells the story of her friendship with the midwife in a small village in Mali, West Africa. Holloway, who spent two years in Mali as a Peace Corps volunteer, learns about the role of women in this part of Africa through working alongside Monique – and eventually begins raising money for a new clinic. (Her campaign has since pulled in more than $40,000.) Published by a textbook publisher in Illinois, the book has sold extremely well – and Holloway's Web site, e-mail list, and Amazon.com reviews have played a big part in that.

★ ★ ★ ★ ★

My particular book is connected to health and education projects in Mali, West Africa. Because of the nature of the book and the work, I went in knowing that I didn't want to have the typical six-week book tour and then just go on to my next thing. I'm in it for the long haul. I want to connect people to womens' lives in West Africa, so they feel like they know people there. When you know someone on a personal basis, you can't turn a blind eye to the problems they face.

The book was published in the fall of 2006. Doing the Web site was terribly important. It went up simultaneously with the publication. My husband has a communications and branding firm. He designed the book cover, and the site. I wanted to put the Web site on the back of the book. The publisher had never done that before.

Competitive analysis. I did a survey of all these different author Web sites, and I had an intern do a survey as well. We looked at authors like Ann Fadiman and Anita Diamant, and saw what they were doing. You start seeing pretty quickly what's standard. I had an event page, a contact page, a page with a book excerpt, and a video. There's also a way to donate to the new clinic through PayPal.

Also, I wanted to give people everything that they'd need to put on a book event. There are high-res photos of me and Monique, a press kit, posters people can easily customize, bookmarks, and so on.

Whenever I'd arrange to speak with book groups, they'd ask me in advance, "Do you have any key questions we should be talking about?" After you get asked that a dozen times, you say, "I really should have one online." [Funding from] the Literary Ventures Fund helped me make a whole kit for book groups, and they also helped with publicity.

Seeding the discussion. I enter every person's e-mail address into a database, so I can send out mass e-mails. I have more than 1,000 names. We use CiviCRM, an open-source database. It's free, and very flexible.

> "I often ask, 'Will you please just post a review of the book, or post about it on your blog?'"

Barnes & Noble picked *Monique* for an online discussion in 2007. When that happened, I e-mailed all the people in the database and said, "I'm going to be on Barnes & Noble online, and I'm not that well-known an author. Please, just ask a question." They did, and that got the discussion going.

People e-mail me and say, "Can I send you a book, and can you sign it and sent it to my sister, who is a midwife?" I do, but I also figure they owe me something. So I often ask, "Will you please just post a review of the book, or post about it on your blog?" I'll send them instructions about how they can post a review on Amazon. The first 20 or 25 reviews there were people I'd asked to post.

Early on, when people e-mailed me, I'd ask them to share an e-mail with five of their friends. And I gave them a little e-mail that they could pass along.

I have a Google Alert set to notify me whenever something goes up on the Web about *Monique and the Mango Rains*.

The book has really taken off in the blogging community. A lot of women in their teens and twenties read it. I'll see that the book is mentioned on a blog, and either in the comments or in an e-mail, I'll reach out to them.

A lot of times, bloggers will e-mail me back and say, "Would you mind doing an interview?" And I don't mind, obviously.

We created a video about the book for YouTube. A good friend of ours works for National Geographic, and my husband did all of his business identity stuff. In return, we got a free video.

The majority of e-mails are people being sweet and saying "thank you." I tried to respond within a week at first, but now my goal is within three weeks. With more complex questions, I try to point people to links, or to my author Q&A on the site. I try to be generous, because if people weren't generous to me, I wouldn't have a book.

Live events. A lot of the events I do are academic, where a student or a professor will contact me: "We're reading your book at school." I also get requests from public libraries and women's groups. It's up to me to ask for an honorarium to make it work. Though I do some events and fund-raisers via speakerphone.

At events, I always capture peoples' e-mail addresses. I used to e-mail everybody after the event: "It was great to meet you, and here's what you can do to get involved with this cause, here's where you can donate, and here's how you can spread the word about the book."

My day job is at the Center for International Studies. We send students overseas to study abroad during their college years.

The advice I'd give to other people is to think about who your audience is, and how they're best reached. And know what you'll keep up with. You start off with a burst of energy, and then you drop it. Start small. Pick the two or three things you're most excited about. For me, it was raising money to build a clinic in Mali, and having that one-to-one contact with readers at events and through e-mail.

Eugene Mirman
Comedian and Writer

Eugene Mirman attended the kind of college where you could declare Comedy as your major – and perform a one-hour stand-up act as your thesis project. The education must have served him well, since he now works as a Brooklyn-based Professional Comedian, opening for bands like Modest Mouse and Cake, playing recurring roles on HBO's "Flight of the Conchords" and the Adult Swim show "Delocated," releasing comedy albums, and touring with the Comedians of Comedy Tour. His first book, *The Will to Whatevs*, was published by HarperCollins in 2009.

★ ★ ★ ★ ★

It used to be that there were three networks, and a handful of record labels. Now, the advantage of the Internet is that it puts much more control in my hands. I do mostly projects that I enjoy, and I work on lots of different things with friends. And you can also get paid for it.

The Internet isn't just a way to promote yourself. It's like television. It is its own medium.

In 1998 or 1999, when I was living in Boston, I worked at a Web consulting firm, Zentropy Partners. I said to the person I shared my office with, "I need to make a Web site." We put up the Singing Baby, and some videos, and suddenly, my Web site became viral. The Singing Baby was a picture of me as a baby, in Russia, and you can hear it sing lots of classic rock songs. I got an e-mail from Pete Townshend one day. Recently, I updated it.

Videos for the Web. The videos weren't like stand-up at all. They were me talking to the camera. At the time, there was one that parodied an IBM ad that I saw on TV. I made that in the bathroom of the Hong Kong, which is a comedy club in Harvard Square where I used to perform a lot.

One was "The Sexpert" [in which Mirman gives extremely bad advice about sex]. If you watched these videos, you'd barely know that I was a comic.

Sure, I listed shows that I was going to do. But the Web site was built in Flash, and it was very difficult for me to update.

When I moved to New York, my success was really a result of Internet word-of-mouth, as opposed to putting out a comedy record. I had done "Conan" once, but the Internet was the first thing that really got me attention.

The most helpful thing was the Singing Baby. It just went around and around. People would recognize me from that. Way more people knew me from that than from TV appearances.

Getting paid. There's two different things. One is making something that's popular, and the other is making money. I used to get tens of thousands of hits on my Web site, and I had no idea how to turn it into anything.

Web companies that wanted content for their sites hired me to make content for them. I produced stuff for SuperDeluxe and 23/6.

> "There's two different things. One is making something that's popular, and the other is making money."

I do several different things. I write, I act, I do stand-up, and I make films. You can now do a hundred different things, and they all come together to form your career.

My videos had been around since 1999. I didn't put any of them on YouTube. Random people would rip them from my site and put them on. Sub Pop, my current label, put some on.

I do have an e-mail list of thousands of people, which is people who sign up at shows or on my site, and I have thousands of MySpace friends. I can post about a show in Boise, Idaho, and have people who have friends in Boise, Idaho tell them to go. That really wasn't possible without the

Internet. On Facebook, I can change my status, and say, "I'm performing in Philadelphia this weekend."

For me, Facebook is more pleasant. On MySpace, I get constant junk from lots of people who want me to listen to their terrible song or sign up for some weird promotion. It has become white noise. I think it will destroy MySpace. Both sites can be effective for promotion. But I have five times the friends on MySpace that I have on Facebook.

Promoting my book. I have a book coming out, and I didn't grow up being known as an author. I want anybody who has seen me perform or knows me from "Flight of the Conchords" to be aware of it. Sure, hopefully blogs will write about the book, but hopefully *Rolling Stone* will give it a good review, and I'll get to promote it on "The Daily Show." You just have to go down as many avenues as possible.

When my first record came out on Suicide Squeeze, they hired a PR person to promote it. I have her doing PR for the book. I also have a manager/agent.

A lot of things fail when you try to hand them over to another company. With my book, I like the people I'm working with a lot, but I've just heard so many horror stories about not being promoted. Then, your book does poorly, and nobody will ever work with you again. So that's why I hired a publicist to be on top of it.

I believe in diversification of income, because you never know what will happen. I'm a slightly paranoid person who thinks things could be ruined at any time. But then when a Web site goes out of business or stops paying for content, which is what happened with SuperDeluxe and 23/6, you're not dependent on them.

I don't really go out to commercial auditions. I would rather spend my time blogging or promoting a show.

I like blogging. I enjoy writing little things and linking to stuff. I like being in touch with people by e-mail. A lot of people want advice. The only advice I have is, you should go do things and try things, and in ten years, you'll most likely succeed.

For me, right now, the volume of e-mail is manageable. But if my special on Comedy Central plays, I'll get five pages of messages, and I can't get to that. Or if I go away for a week, that's kind of unmanageable.

Taking control. In comedy, there used to be so many people who would perform at a showcase for the industry. People would say, "You're funny, but I have no idea what to do with you. I don't know how to book you or put you in something." Now, you can take control of it yourself. My career doesn't depend on whether FX can figure out where to put me, and you don't have to have a company selling you in some way that you don't like. That's one of the great things about the Internet.

The whole thing is, you're freelancing. If you expect that some big company will swoop in and give you a bunch of money and make you a star – that's a flawed business model.

> "People would say, 'You're funny, but I have no idea what to do with you. I don't know how to book you or put you in something.' Now, you can take control of it yourself."

My book will be out in February 2009, and I will have a CD out in the summer of 2009 from Sub Pop, and I'm working on a documentary about going back to Russia for the first time, which Michael Showalter is going to direct.

I live in a small apartment in Brooklyn. I haven't figured out how to build an empire. I've just figured out how to do shows I enjoy, write books, and enjoy my career. The Internet is wildly helpful for that.

Dan and Dave Buck
Pioneers of Extreme Card Manipulation

 Dave and Dan Buck are two of the pioneers of a dazzling card-handling style called Extreme Card Manipulation (XCM), or flourishes. They put out their first videotape while still in high school, and now the brothers, both in their mid-20s, run a popular community site for people interested in XCM, DanAndDave.com. Originally from the rural town of Sonoma, California, they now live in Hollywood and lecture and teach around the world. A prominent part of their site is an online store where visitors can buy books and videos created by Dan and Dave and other magicians.

★ ★ ★ ★ ★

Dan Buck: Our community on the Web site is our sole income. It has really grown into a business. We started our Web site in high school. We had made a quick home video teaching some material. We sold it through PayPal. We saved every dime we could and went to these magic conventions. We'd perform, and do our stuff, and advertise our site.

Dave Buck: We made that first video one morning before school. We borrowed our parents' eight-millimeter video camera and shot it in like two hours. There was no editing. We filmed it all in one take – just press record, press stop, then do the next bit. It was two hours long, really raw. We were about fifteen years old at the time. We had a neighbor three doors down who could duplicate videotapes. He charged us $10 a tape, and we sold them for $35.

Dan: The material on it was a new style – what people call flourishes or extreme card manipulation. It mimics poetry. We grew up in Sonora, two hours east of San Francisco. There was nothing to do. We saw magic on TV and decided that's what we wanted to do. So we just practiced all the time, and came up with new and original material.

We sold a couple hundred copies of that first tape. For kids, it was pretty good. In 2002, we redid that on DVD, and we've sold close to 10,000. We produce the videos and edit them ourselves. We also started producing our friends who do magic, making their DVDs. It became this full-time business.

Our entire Web site was made by the two of us. But last July [2008], we decided to get a new Web site, and we hired a professional firm of Web developers to do some of the more complicated Web programming. We're always releasing something new on the Web site, and we update it often, to force people to come back and see the new information, get the latest news.

Dave: We got into this new art form of flourishes at the perfect time, right around its birth. When others started their sites, everyone credited back to us and linked to us.

> "When we'd go to conventions in the early days, we'd just sit in the lobby all day and sell DVDs..."

Our art is such a visual art that we can just walk in and do what we do. When we'd go to conventions in the early days, we'd just sit in the lobby all day and sell DVDs and videos and lecture notes from our backpacks. We put our Web site address on everything, and we'd tell people about the forums on our site.

Dan: We'd buy the plane ticket, but many times we couldn't afford the convention itself. We'd sneak in if we could. But all the action happens in the lobby anyway.

Dave: Our best-selling product is definitely our three DVD box set. It sells for $85, and we just broke 10,000 in sales in less than two years. I think it has gone down in the magic industry as the highest-grossing product out there. We started with 6,000 copies, which cost us $35,000 to produce. We made that back within the first 24 hours.

Up until July of 2008, we fulfilled every order ourselves. But now, we go through a fulfillment house out of New York.

Instead of having a trailer or a preview for that DVD set, we released about ten minutes of footage in total from all three DVDs. We allowed our community to edit together a trailer on their own. We had about 70 submissions. A normal magic DVD has only one preview video, and here we had 70, plastered all across the Internet. The winning trailers will be on our next DVD, "andthensome."

Dan: There was a rating system so that members of our community could rate the videos. It wasn't us who chose the winners.

On our forums, we find that sales drop and visits drop when we don't participate. So we're on every day for at least an hour. We always create new contests and give away prizes. Last month, we had a playing card collection contest. The guy with the best collection of playing cards won a $50 gift certificate. We're always doing something to generate traffic.

If people have problems with a trick, they post about their problems, and others suggest things. Or people post about the videos they have up on YouTube.

We sell ten times more DVDs on the site than books. The books generally don't sell.

Dave: Video on demand is becoming our #1 source of revenue. We think that will be our sole business in two or three years. We hired a Web developer to build a system that allows us to upload a performance, and people can instantly watch and purchase it. It goes into their account, under "My Purchases." It's streaming video, so people keep coming back to our site to watch it, rather than a downloadable QuickTime file. If it was downloadable, we think it'd get plastered all over YouTube and the Torrent [file-sharing] sites.

Dan: And we don't have to pay for the printing of the product. There are no delays or shipping problems to deal with.

We do have a mailing list of a little more than 2,000 people. We send out a newsletter at least once a month, sometimes two times. It's something we started doing over the last year. It's not as big a group of people as those who participate in our forums.

Recently, we started lecturing. It has been very profitable for us. We did three lectures in France for $12,000, and a tour in Asia made us about $9,000. We did some consulting for an Icelandic TV show for kids, and we were hand doubles for a film called *Smoking Aces*.

The Web site is probably 65 or 70 percent of our income, and most of that is from DVD sales.

Dave: The first of every month, we release a new product that's limited and can only be bought through our site. We'll find some rare cards and buy them all. We had fifty copies of *Genii* magazine [which we were in], and we signed them all. We sold the uncut sheets of our playing cards, signed.

> "The first of every month, we release a new product that's limited and can only be bought through our site."

Dan: We're creating an Academy section of the site, where we're going to have free videos for newcomers, people interested in learning some basic things. If they learn the basics, and they want to advance, then they'll inevitably wind up paying for some videos.

Dave: We're going to Blackpool, England in February 2009 to do thirteen shows, at a big magic convention. But performing has never been something we're passionate about. We love developing new ideas, rather than performing the same effect over and over.

We've just continued to do what we love, and everything sort of followed. It all started with that first video we made in high school, and grew into a business. When we tell people what we do, they say, "Where do you perform?" It's difficult to describe how we make a living.

Now, we have to pay to get into conventions, because people know who we are. Not paying would be just incredibly tacky.

Mark Day
Comedian and YouTube Executive

In the early days of YouTube, Mark Day carved out a reputation online as the Scottish Dennis Miller. Day, who had a "fairly boring" day job at a Bay Area advertising agency, posted one comedic rant a week to the site, and most attracted more than 30,000 views. Day felt like he was reaching more people, and getting more feedback, than he did when he performed at small stand-up clubs, so he stopped performing almost entirely to focus on the videos. He became one of the highest-profile comedians on the site, and was an early participant in YouTube's "Partner Program," where the site cuts creators in on advertising revenues. In 2008, he landed a job at YouTube, as a liaison who works with the site's content partners.

★ ★ ★ ★ ★

I had gotten interested in stand-up, mostly because someone else I knew was doing it, and I said, "Wait a minute – I'm funnier than he is." I quickly discovered that the world of stand-up comedy is a very long and very involving apprenticeship. It takes a willingness to schlep around to cafés that are willing to let new comics try out. Or you have to run your own comedy night somewhere, so you can trade off favors with other comedians. It seemed like something I should've done ten years earlier, or that I just shouldn't expect that much from.

But as soon as I started performing stand-up comedy, I set up a MySpace page, and I was vaguely aware of YouTube as a place that would host your videos. I worked in an office, at a business-to-business advertising firm. You could see what would happen when everyone would gather around someone's desk to watch videos on the Internet. I vaguely started to grasp the idea that if something happened that was newsworthy and noteworthy, and you were one of the first to make a video about it, you had a reasonable chance that people would watch it.

One of my first videos was based on this news item about someone who recorded their attempt to cancel their AOL account. In it, I was attempting to cancel my Playboy subscription. A lot of people saw it, compared to the twelve bored comedians who listened to my stuff at open mic nights. It was a fun way to get my opinions out there, without having to suck up to local comedians to get on their shows.

Posting everywhere. Any time I stumbled across a new video site that was starting up, I'd dump all of my videos there. Sometimes, a lot of people would see them. And sometimes, you'd go back and no one would have seen them. I posted on a site called Revver, and made a couple hundred dollars, because they shared advertising revenue with you.

But that strategy must have worked, because some people told me, "I just kept seeing your videos everywhere, so I eventually succumbed to clicking on your picture to see what it was about."

I started to learn that the thumbnail image for your video was important. Does it pop off the page? I'd painted my home office with this bright yellow color, and the thumbnail was always my head in front of that wall.

Finding the right frequency. I settled into a pace of doing one video a week, just because that seemed doable. Often, the happiest I was was the day after I made a video, because I didn't have to do that again for another six days. But if I didn't feed the machine and get new subscribers to replenish the people who got bored, I felt like I was somehow going to disappear from view.

I discovered at one point that if I said at the end of the video, "Rate this video," more people would. And if enough of them did, my videos would show up at the top of the most-rated list, so that kept me visible. I'd encourage people to come up with their own rating system and leave it in the comments below my videos, to try to create an opportunity for people to interact and feel like they have a stake in it. They're not just passively watching, but they're being funny back at me.

I also created some merchandise and sold it on CafePress, which brought in a couple hundred bucks.

I was lucky to come along and make videos at a time when not so many other people were doing it. But I also put a lot of thought into the presentation and the frequency and all the things that made it feel more like a regular show. But it's a hell of a lot harder for anyone to get noticed today.

What were the benefits of doing it? The biggest reward was doing something creative that was just for me. I got endless requests from Internet video start-ups who desperately wanted me to somehow migrate my subscribers over to their sites. But nothing that was appealing enough to cut myself off from the YouTube ecosystem.

Focusing on YouTube. As I said, I had a MySpace page. But after a while, I was trying to drive people from MySpace to watch my videos on YouTube, and rate them and post comments. It's best to aggregate your views on the site where you want people to be.

> "If you make yourself something of an expert, in the process of distributing your content online, you may find opportunities to develop your career..."

If you make yourself something of an online expert, in the process of distributing your content online, you may find opportunities to develop your career on both sides of the camera, as it were. I found opportunities to consult here and there.

I eventually went to work for a Web site called Rooftop Comedy, which specializes in stand-up comedy clips. Knowing about comedy on the Web certainly helped me get that job. I could point to a lot of things I'd done in video. While I was there, I would interact with a lot of people from traditional comedy backgrounds, who made their living traveling around to clubs. A lot of them don't see the obvious payoff of creating stuff for the Web, or they think it's something they should be doing, but see it as an enormous time suck. Their idea of a career in comedy was that you toured around, eventually you moved to LA, and then you got a job in a writing room for a sitcom while you were waiting to get your own sitcom. You get paid at most steps in that process, which just isn't true with the Web.
And they worry about whether they're devaluing their work by giving it away for free. And are you putting youself back down on the same level as

your audience, rather than being elevated above it. Those may be barriers for people.

Ad revenue. When YouTube started the Partner Program [which shares with creators some of the advertising revenue their videos generate], I was one of the first people in the pilot. The money was more gravy for me than anything else. I recently bought a second car, and making videos paid for that car. It allowed me to buy consumer electronics, and write them off on my taxes. It was never my full-time job, but I made reasonable money.

One day in 2007, I came to YouTube for a brown bag lunch. The community team was having local users come in in small groups to ask questions about likes and dislikes, how we used the site. I met some people in the company. Then, when there was an opening here, one of the employees said that I should submit my résumé. It was the same rigorous Google interview process as everyone else goes through. [Google is YouTube's parent company.] But I think when the opportunity came along, I had a particularly good set of experience that not a lot of other people had. I started in January 2008, helping our content partners understand the community — what works here and what doesn't work. I've gotten to go to the Just for Laughs festival in Montreal, to speak on a panel, and to LA for the media launch of Seth MacFarlane's Cavalcade of Comedy. It's great fun.

I burned out after a year of making my videos. It was kind of a relief for me to drop off the YouTube most-subscribed users list, and no longer just wonder when that would happen. Now I just make them when I feel inspired to say something.

Anyone who is serious about building their online audience has to recognize that the tools for doing that are not frozen in time and space in 2006, or 2007. Having a MySpace page that takes forever to load because it's covered in baubles and HTML gewgaws is only worth so much to you if you don't know how to set up a Facebook group, or haven't started working your Twitter ID into your fan communications.

Exploring the
New Business Models

In the past, the tried-and-true business model for artists – the way they reliably made money – was to get an advance from a record label or publisher, and then produce something. If the product was a hit, the royalties would stream in (minus any marketing or promotional spending done on your behalf). If the product flopped, the next advance shrank considerably, or wasn't offered at all.

That model isn't exactly facing extinction, but new models are emerging, some of which will work much better for some artists. Many of these models eliminate layers of middlemen who each shave off their own slice of the profits.

This isn't a comprehensive list of every revenue model that can support your career; rather, it's intended to get you thinking. You may discover something that works better for you.

> Merchandise

Most artists I spoke with for this book earn most of their income from selling physical stuff, whether it's books, DVDs, CDs, or prints or originals of their artwork. Some add a small premium to the price of this stuff when they autograph it, or sell limited-edition merchandise.

There are three ways to sell physical goods. The first, and least profitable, is to have a service like CreateSpace or CafePress make it for your customers on an "on demand" basis. That means there is no up-front investment for you, and you don't have to guess how many copies of your new CD people will want to purchase. Every time someone buys your CD,

CreateSpace cranks out a new one and ships it out for you. If you sell a $20 CD directly from your CreateSpace e-store (linking the buyer there from your Web site, for instance), you keep about $12. But if you sell a $20 CD through Amazon.com (CreateSpace's parent company), you keep just $4.

The second way, slightly more profitable, is to make your own merchandise in batches, and have a fulfillment house handle orders for you. You might make 500 DVDs, for instance, and then send them to Film Baby or Neoflix. At Neoflix, after paying a one-time set-up charge ($238) and a monthly fee ($35), the company takes just 12 percent of every sale. So a $20 DVD would net you $17.60. The danger, of course, is that you may over-produce your merchandise and be left with unsold stuff.

The third and most profitable approach is to make your own merchandise in batches and fulfill it yourself (or pay a part-time employee or intern to handle fulfillment.) You might collect orders through your site, and package up your outgoing shipments once or twice a week and taking them to the post office. The only overhead costs here are postage and packaging materials – and, of course, your time. There's still the danger of over-producing, and the slightly higher hassle factor of handling returns and customer service yourself.

> Digital Downloads

You'll almost definitely want to sell digital versions of your work, whether it's in MP3, MP4, MOV, WMV, or PDF form. Most artists price the digital version at a lower level than the physical product.

Some, like the band Radiohead and the documentary filmmaker Hunter Weeks, have experimented with letting purchasers set their own price for the digital download. Radiohead said its fans paid about as much as their album, "In Rainbows," cost at retail. (But a study by the research firm comScore found that only 38 percent of customers paid for the album, with the rest downloading it for free. That study found the average price paid by those who did open their wallets was $6.) Weeks tried his experiment after several months selling fixed-price downloads at $7.99, and said people paid between $3 and $4 when they were able to name their own price.

An important choice is whether you want your digital files to be copy-protected, or enclosed in a DRM (digital rights management) wrapper, which makes them tougher for people to trade with one another, but can also make them harder for one person to use on multiple PCs or devices. iTunes, for instance, seems to be moving away from DRM-protected music files and toward more flexible MP3 files, though the videos it sells are still packaged with DRM. Amazon's digital downloads are similar: music is sold without DRM, but video includes Windows Media copy protection. Books can be sold as plain old PDFs, which have no DRM, or copy-protected PDFs. Other formats, like the books sold for Amazon's Kindle e-book reader, also have copy-protection built in. But the Kindle is also able to display regular, non-copy-protected PDFs.

Downloads can be sold two ways. The first is through a marketplace like iTunes, Amazon, or YouTube (which in 2009 began testing a paid download service with some content partners.) Typically, the creator will get about 70 percent of the revenue from those arrangements. The upside is that these marketplaces attract lots of traffic, so there's a good chance that people who may not know about your work will discover it there.

A more profitable way to sell downloads is directly through your own site, using a service like E-Junkie. E-Junkie charges a low monthly fee, starting at $5 per month, to enable digital downloads of any kind of file: a PDF e-book, a QuickTime movie, or an MP3 song. PayLoadz, a similar service, permits up to $100 worth of transactions for free, after which monthly fees start at $15. But the only people who will find your work this way are people who've already arrived at your site.

In addition to downloads, which the user owns upon purchase, services like Rhapsody and Imeem effectively "rent" music to listeners by streaming it, and iTunes, Amazon, and Jaman can offer time-limited digital rentals of videos.

> Speaking, Workshops and Seminars

Many artists who've developed expertise around new approaches to production, distribution, and marketing find that others want to tap into that expertise. They're invited to speak at conferences, to college classes, or at meetings of industry networking groups.

Some view these invitations simply as an opportunity to meet new people, share what they know, and build up their brand. And that's OK.

Others may choose to develop presentations or workshops that offer insight into their creative process, the tools they use, or the new ways they interact with their audience - and charge a speaker's fee for delivering them (or at least have their travel expenses covered, giving them a chance to visit exotic locales).

In cultivating this sort of income, it helps to have a page on your Web site that lists the presentations you give (and perhaps also includes audio, video, and quotes from people who've seen you in action.) You may opt to be represented by a speaker's bureau or agent who will help market you in exchange for a percentage of your fees, or you may want to book engagements yourself. (Sometimes, speaker's bureaus will turn down offers that are "too small" - IE, not a big enough commission for them - that you might want to accept.) Filmmaker Sandi DuBowski and video artist Ze Frank are both represented by speaker's bureaus; Frank, artist Tracy White, and videoblogger Steve Garfield are among those who've also dabbled in teaching college courses related to their work.

A worthy area of exploration is doing presentations or workshops via videoconference, using a tool like Skype or iChat. That eliminates the costs of travel, which lets you charge a smaller fee and spend your time more effectively.

> Ad Splits and Revenue Shares

Earning money from advertising placed around (or in) your content works well only when you're generating a consistently high volume of plays, visits, or views. Sites like Imeem, Metacafe, and YouTube offer "partner programs" where content creators can earn a slice of the revenue from graphic ads placed next to their content, or ads inserted into it. Sometimes, you're earning a little bit every time an ad is shown, and sometimes, you get paid only when someone clicks.

To start earning substantial sums, you'll need to generate hundreds of thousands or millions of plays. One YouTube video creator whose work, a sitcom called "Break a Leg," had been seen about two million times reported being paid just $1600; on Revver, another revenue-sharing site, a hit video called "Extreme Diet Coke and Mentos Experiments" was seen more than 10 million times and earned its two creators $50,000. Michael Buckley, a YouTube performer whose videos are regularly seen by about 200,000 people (and who is one of the top ten "most subscribed" channels on the site), reported earning more than $100,000 a year from ad revenue sharing.

Google's AdSense program will enable you to integrate text, graphical, and even video ads into your Web site and then send you a portion of the revenue those ads generate. Other ad networks, like AdBrite, AzoogleAds, Burst! Media, BlueLithium, and Federated Media, offer similar ad placement services. Some of them prefer to work only with sites that have already established a large audience. Extremely popular sites can earn significant sums: AskTheBuilder.com reportedly brings in about $30,000 a month, and blogs like ShoeMoney.com and Boing Boing earn even more.

Sites like Amazon, iTunes, and Netflix operate "affiliate programs" where they will send revenue your way in exchange for your sending them paying customers. Netflix, for instance, pays you a $9 bounty for every person who signs up for a free trial. Amazon's Associates Program will pay you a percentage of a customer's total shopping cart purchase, even if you've just pointed them to your book, CD, or DVD on the site. Signing up for these programs is simple – and free.

> Tip Jars

Visitors to your site may want to express their appreciation, so why not give them an opportunity to slide you a buck or two? Some artists choose to give away some material for free, like a demo song or a PDF e-book, and let visitors know that tips are welcome. Some of the options for accepting tips are TipJoy, ScratchBack, TipIt, and PayPal's donation mechanism.

> Online Project Funding/Donations

In the place of advances, some more established artists are finding that they can raise money online from people who are familiar with their work, or aligned with a political or social cause that they're engaged with. (This strategy can be extremely challenging for your first album, book, or film.) The documentary filmmaker Robert Greenwald raised more than $200,000 online for his 2006 documentary *Iraq for Sale*, which explored questions of war profiteering in that country. Songwriter Jill Sobule raised nearly $90,000 for her 2009 album, *California Years*, by holding a virtual telethon on the site Jillsnextrecord.com. Sites like Fundable, ArtistShare, and IndieGoGo provide support for online project funding. Before diving in, it's wise to find out who has raised money successfully using a given service, how much, and why they were successful at it.

> Subscriptions/Clubs/Membership

If you have a devoted enough group of fans, or you are producing some sort of continuing content that has exceptional value to it, you may be able to create a subscription area to your site and charge a monthly or yearly fee. (In the "Power Tools" section of the book, I've listed some of the services that will support you in selling subscriptions.) One challenge is that you've got to promise and deliver special benefits to this group of subscribers to keep them happy, and get them to renew after their first term runs out.

Many sites that offer textual tips and information (like knitting patterns, stock market advice, or fitness training guidance) can and do charge subscriptions.

The creators of the animated series "Red vs. Blue" charge $10 for a six month membership to the site, which gives members access to new episodes a few days early, and offers all sorts of bonus materials. They're also prominently identified on the site as supporters of the series.

Long-established bands like KISS, The Who, and U2 offer membership on their sites, at about $50 per year. Benefits include things like exclusive video, merchandise discounts, dispatches from the road, and early access to special ticket blocks.

Director David Lynch (*Eraserhead, Wild at Heart*) sells a $10 per month membership to his site, which has served up original video series like "Dumbland," and also given members the chance to e-mail questions to Lynch while he was at the Cannes Film Festival and have him answer them in a video. And of course, George Lucas runs an online "Star Wars" fan club, for $14.95 a year, giving members access to special newsletters, merchandise discounts, sneak previews of upcoming projects, and early notice about upcoming fan events.

> Sponsorship/Underwriting/Product Placement

Novels, concert tours, Internet videos, and films have all taken advantage of sponsorship, underwriting and product placement to help cover their expenses.

When Fay Weldon wrote the novel *The Bulgari Connection*, published in 2001, the high-end jeweler paid her £18,000 in exchange for mentioning their brand at least a dozen times in the text. Author Sean Stewart did a similar product placement deal with Cover Girl Cosmetics (though the product mentions were dropped when his book came out in paperback.)

Indie filmmaker Hunter Weeks sold several sponsorships of his 2008 film *10 Yards*, about fantasy football, to companies like Crocs and Quiznos. (Quiznos funded a weekend in Las Vegas as a contest prize.) Welch's grape juice sponsored a documentary called *A Hero for Daisy*, about the campaign for equality in women's collegiate athletics, and the apparel-maker Vans helped fund Stacy Peralta's skateboarding doc *Dogtown and Z-Boys*.

The 2008 documentary *I.O.U.S.A.* was purchased outright – not just underwritten – by the Peter G. Peterson Foundation, which sought to use the doc to promote fiscal responsibility.

YouTube videomakers like the chipmunk-voiced teenager Fred (who has 585,000 subscribers to his channel) have woven in product placements to their videos, hawking new movies or consumer electronics. Other YouTube stars, like iJustine, have been hired by companies like AT&T and Mozy to create Web ad campaigns for their products.

A few services, like Brandfame and Digital Content Partners, exist to connect Web video producers with product placement opportunities. But in most cases, if you are interested in selling sponsorships or product placements for your book, film, or world tour, you'll have to approach the companies or non-profits you think might be interested – or have your agent do it on your behalf.

> Venture Capital

Venture capitalists are professional investors who funnel money – typically millions of dollars – into businesses they think could turn into the next Apple, Google, or Amazon.

While a few of them may invest as individuals in films or recording projects, that is much more the exception than the rule. Unless you know of a specific venture capitalist with a history of doing this, don't waste your time.

But VCs may be interested if you have an idea to build a set of tools that may be useful to other artists; a distribution or marketing platform that others can benefit from; or a new kind of studio that will support the creative efforts of dozens or hundreds of artists. They've supported companies like the animation studio JibJab, Avid Technology, the developer of video editing tools; video sites like YouTube, Blip.tv, and Veoh; the comedy site Funny or Die, created by Will Ferrell and Adam McKay; and Harmonix Music Systems, the company that originally developed "Guitar Hero" and later created "Rock Band." Venture capitalists want to see a solid business plan. They need to believe that you and your team can build a big, important company. And they eventually want to cash out by taking your company public or selling it to someone else – which can create incredible pressure for everyone involved.

Power Tools for Audience-Building, Collaboration and Commerce

Here are some of the tools that successful artists rely on to build and connect with their online fan base – and earn a living doing it. This isn't a comprehensive list of every useful tool, or every tool in a specific category (there are dozens of different services that will host blogs, for instance.) Rather, I've tried to focus on the tools that artists have most frequently cited as useful, those I have personal experience using, and those that are free or cheap. Wherever there is a fee for using a tool, I've noted that.

> Venues, Booking & Tours

BookTour
http://www.booktour.com
Helps authors promote live events, and connects book groups, libraries and other organizations with authors willing to speak.

Brave New Theaters
http://bravenewtheaters.com
Connects filmmakers with groups and individuals who organize communal "house party"-style screenings around the country.

Demand It
http://eventful.com/demand/learn
Allows fans to "demand" (request, really) that performers come to their town. Performers can see where large numbers of their fans are concentrated, schedule gigs there, and communicate directly with fans in that area to get them to show up.

Sonicbids
http://www.sonicbids.com
Connects musicians with venues. $5.95 per month.

> Blogging & Micro-blogging

Blogger
http://www.blogger.com
Google-operated free blogging service. Very easy to get started, but features and design templates are somewhat limited. If you own your own Web domain (like coolguy.com), you can have the blog published to that site, rather than using a Blogger domain (coolguy.blogspot.com).

FeedBlitz
http://www.feedblitz.com/f/?Newsletter
Allows visitors to your blog to subscribe to an e-mail update service, so they receive an e-mail whenever new content is posted. Allows you to view your list of subscribers, and export their e-mail addresses for other communications. $9.98 per month for 100-499 subscribers, $13.95 per month for 500-999 subscribers.

Feedburner
http://www.feedburner.com
Tool for creating RSS feeds of your blog or podcast, so that readers can keep current with it using their favorite RSS reader software. Also keeps track of how many subscribers your RSS feed has, and allows you to insert advertising into the feed to earn money. Owned by Google, so it's free.

Posterous
http://posterous.com
Aimed at being the simplest kind of blog to set up (albeit with limited features), all you do is send an e-mail to post@posterous.com and you've instantly got a blog. Whenever you e-mail a photo, link, MP3, or video file, Posterous intelligently formats it or puts it in a player so it's easily experienced. Free, with storage of up to one gigabyte.

Tumblr
http://www.tumblr.com

Free blogging service with simplified set-up and posting, geared to short posts, Web site links, photos, and videos.

Twitter
http://twitter.com
"Micro-blogging" service that limits posts to 140 characters. Some people use Twitter in addition to maintaining a blog, and some use it instead of having a blog. You can Twitter from just about any mobile phone, or your computer. Anyone can choose to follow your Twitter updates (known as "tweets"), and you'll be able to see how many "followers" you have through the site – and who they are. Your followers can also leave comments on your Twitter posts, or re-tweet them, publishing them as part of their own Twitter stream to share them with their own followers.

Wordpress
http://www.wordpress.com
More sophisticated and flexible blogging service. Basic version is free, but if you need more storage, want your blog to live at your own domain (like coolguy.com), or want to be sure ads aren't shown on your blog, you'll pay an annual fee (from $10 on up.)

> Traffic & Analytics

Alexa
http://www.alexa.com
Enables you to get an estimate of any Web site's traffic. Very useful when trying to figure out which Web sites you should target as promotional partners. Also allows you to compare the audience "reach" of one Web site to another.

Compete
http://www.compete.com
Enables you to get an estimate of any Web site's traffic. Very useful when trying to figure out which Web sites you should target as promotional partners. Also allows you to compare the audience "reach" or popularity of one Web site to another.

Google Alerts
http://www.google.com/alerts

Enter any term – like your band's name, or the title of your book – and Google will keep tabs on who is talking about it anywhere on the Web, and e-mail you a daily or weekly alert. Vital service for keeping tabs on where your work is being discussed or reviewed.

Google Analytics
http://www.google.com/analytics
Free tools for measuring and analyzing the traffic that comes to your Web site or blog.

Site Meter
http://www.sitemeter.com
Tools for measuring and analyzing the traffic that comes to your Web site or blog. Basic version is free; advanced version starts at $6.95.

Website Grader
http://website.grader.com
Website Grader is a free service that evaluates how welcoming your Web site is to search engines – and thus how high you'll appear in lists of search results

> Commerce & Distribution

Amazon
http://www.amazonservices.com/content/sell-on-amazon.htm
http://www.amazonservices.com/content/fulfillment-by-amazon.htm
http://www.amazonservices.com/content/amazon-checkout-payments.htm
Everyone's familiar with Amazon as a consumer-oriented e-commerce site. But Amazon also offers a program for sellers, letting you place CDs, DVDs, books, or other products you produce on the site (in exchange for a monthly fee and a per-purchase piece of the action). And Amazon will also fulfill orders for you, storing your merchandise and sending it out when someone orders (also a monthly fee and a per-order charge.) There's also an Amazon Payments service, which lets you place a button on your Web site and has Amazon handle the payment process and forward the money to you (similar to the way Google Checkout and PayPal work.)

AmieStreet
http://amiestreet.com

Site dedicated to helping listeners discover new music. All songs start off by either being free or priced inexpensively. As music becomes more popular, the price to download it rises. After you sell more than $5 worth of downloads, you keep 70 percent of all revenues.

Artist Rising
http://www.artistrising.com
Sell prints and posters of your artwork through Art.com (Artist Rising's parent company), produced on demand, and receive a 15 percent royalty. Basic membership is free; premium costs $50 per year.

Brown Paper Tickets
http://www.brownpapertickets.com/producers.html
Online ticketing service that will work with any venue... from a warehouse where you're screening your film to a club you've rented for a record release concert. Customers pay a small fee – 99 cents and 2.5 percent of the ticket price – but event producers pay nothing.

CafePress
http://www.cafepress.com/cp/customize/
Free service that allows you to design your own custom mugs, calendars, t-shirts, or other products, and will produce them on demand as your fans order them. You promote the merch, and CafePress sends you a percentage of every purchase.

CD Baby
http://www.cdbaby.com
Sell CDs and digital downloads on iTunes, Amazon, Rhapsody, and other sites. (You send them CDs to sell.) $35 set-up fee. CD Baby keeps $4 from the purchase price every CD sold and 9 percent from every digital sale. (CD Baby can also sell audio books.)

CreateSpace
https://www.createspace.com/
A division of Amazon.com. Enables you to publish books, CDs, DVDs, and audio and video downloads. Products are manufactured on demand, and can be sold through a CreateSpace storefront linked from your site (which offers better profit margins) or through Amazon.com.

E-Junkie
http://www.e-junkie.com/
Shopping cart software for selling digital and physical merchandise. Automatically calculates shipping and stores digital files for instant download, with no bandwidth limitations or per-transaction fees. Monthly fees start at $5.

Eventbrite
http://www.eventbrite.com
Service for either collecting registration info from people who will attend a free event you're organizing, or charging people to attend a paid event like a seminar or concert. Free to use for free events, but there's a 2.5 percent fee for paid events. Minimum charge of 99 cents per ticket, maximum charge of $9.95. Also enables you to send e-mails to attendees.

Film Baby
http://www.filmbaby.com
Service for selling DVDs. Distributes through Film Baby Web site, Netflix, and to retailers, through partnerships with Ryko Distribution and Super D. Filmmaker gets to keep an average of 80 percent of the sale price, according to the company. You send them DVDs to sell.

Google Checkout
https://checkout.google.com
Payment processing. Similar to PayPal. Allows you to accept Mastercard, Visa, AmEx, and other credit cards on your site. Offers discounts on fees if you also advertise through Google's AdWords program.

Imagekind
http://www.imagekind.com/sell
Will produce prints, posters, and greeting cards of your artwork, on demand. You can set your own price, and you keep 100 percent of the mark-up beyond the item's production price. Basic account on Imagekind is free. Owned by CafePress (see above.)

Independent Online Distribution Alliance
http://www.iodalliance.com/
Distributes music and ringtones to all the major digital music services and mobile carriers, including iTunes, Amazon, Napster, Sprint, and Virgin Mobile. Increasingly handling video/film distribution as well.

iStockPhoto
http://www.istockphoto.com/
Sell photos through this site to Web designers, ad agencies, and publications. Earn a royalty of 20 to 40 percent of the price of each photo downloaded by the site's users. You can sell video and audio here, too.

iUniverse
http://www.iuniverse.com/
Self-publishing service for books, with distribution to sites like Amazon.com, Booksamillion.com, and Barnesandnnoble.com. Good publishing service for authors who want editorial and design assistance, and access to telephone customer support (unlike Lulu and CreateSpace). But book publishing packages start at $599.

Lulu
http://www.lulu.com
No up-front fees. Manufactures CDs, books, and DVDs on demand and sells them to your fans, sharing a percentage of the revenue with you. Can issue ISBN numbers and ensure that books are available for special order by bookstores and libraries, and on e-commerce sites like Amazon.com and Barnesandnoble.com.

Neoflix
http://www.neoflix.com/services
You make the DVDs, and Neoflix helps you sell them online. In return for paying a set-up fee and a monthly service charge, Neoflix allows you to keep a very substantial chunk of the sale price of every DVD. Shopping cart can be linked to your Web site. Products also appear on Amazon.com.

PayLoadz
https://www.payloadz.com
Enables you to sell digital files on your own Web site, with payment via PayPal or Google Checkout. Service is free if you sell under $100 of downloads per month; after that, fees start at $15 per month. An alternative is to avoid the monthly fee and pay PayLoadz 15 percent per transaction.

PayPal
https://www.paypal.com
https://micropayments.paypal-labs.com

Payment system with basic shopping cart software that allows you to accept credit cards on your site (or direct transfers from shoppers' PayPal accounts). Note that if you are selling low-dollar-value items (under $10), you should explore PayPal's Micropayments offering, which charges you less per transaction.

Pump Audio
http://www.pumpaudio.com/artists
Pump pimps your music to ad agencies and TV and film producers. You receive 50 percent of the licensing fees Pump collects from your work. Non-exclusive deal. You retain all rights. Owned by Getty Images.

Tunecore
http://www.tunecore.com
Handles digital distribution of music and music videos to stores and services like Rhapsody, Amazon, iTunes, and eMusic. Charges storage fees (for example, $9.99 per song per year) instead of taking a cut of your profits. As of 2008, starting to distribute indie films and concert films.

Yahoo Merchant Solutions
http://smallbusiness.yahoo.com/ecommerce/index.php
Shopping cart and e-commerce software for selling physical goods, processing payment, and calculating shipping costs. You fulfill orders. Initial set-up fee is $50, plus $39.95 per month and 1.5 percent fee on every purchase.

> Social Networks

Facebook
http://www.facebook.com
http://www.facebook.com/advertising/?pages
It's probably a bad idea to blend your personal Facebook account with that of your artistic career. To keep the two things separate, you can create a "fan page" for your professional persona, your band, or a new project. Your individual Facebook profile will only allow you to have 5,000 friends; a fan page has no such limits. Facebook also allows you to send messages to all your fans. And when people become a fan of your latest project, all their friends will receive an update informing them of that important fact.

MySpace
http://www.myspace.com
MySpace was the first social networking site to really take off, and some consider a profile there to still be a good idea. But as of early 2009, Facebook had more than twice as much traffic worldwide as MySpace (200 million unique users per month to MySpace's 100 million), and it was growing much more quickly. In the US, MySpace still has more traffic, but analysts expect Facebook to surpass it by early 2010.

Ning
http://www.ning.com
Set up your own free social network, with a blog, photo albums, video, chat, discussion forums, e-mail bulletins, calendars, and more.

> Wikis & Collaboration

Wetpaint
http://www.wetpaint.com
Hosts wikis, online spaces where you can collaborate and share ideas with fans. Free.

Wikispaces
http://www.wikispaces.com
Hosts wikis, online spaces where you can collaborate and share ideas with fans. Free version allows you to store up to two megabytes of documents; paid versions start at $5 per month.

Wreck A Movie
http://www.wreckamovie.com
Ignore this Web site's unfortunate name... it's simply a tool created by the team behind the sci-fi parody *Star Wreck*. WreckAMovie is an open and free platform for collaboration between filmmakers and their community, inviting community members to help out with certain tasks.

> Audio

Cinch
http://cinch.blogtalkradio.com

Call a phone number to record audio files, which are recorded as MP3s. Cinch creates an RSS feed that people can subscribe to in any RSS reader, which will deliver your latest recording to them.

Foneshow
http://www.foneshow.com
If you have a podcast series, this free service allows people to subscribe using just about any mobile phone. Subscribers get a text message whenever you publish new content, and they hear the content by dialing a phone number included in the text message. Eliminates the hassles that often surrounding syncing an MP3 player to get the latest podcast content.

FreeConferenceCall.com
http://www.freeconferencecall.com
Want to run a monthly telephonic Q&A with your fans, or brainstorm with a far-flung team about your next release? Use this. Accommodates up to 96 callers on calls lasting up to six hours. Calls can also be recorded and easily turned into podcasts. Free, though there's a fee to host larger groups of callers or to offer callers an 800 number.

Gabcast
http://www.gabcast.com/index.php?a=info&b=overview#
Record audio content for your Web site, or a series of podcasts, simply by dialing a phone number. Free version will store up to 200 megabytes of audio; more sophisticated versions with more storage start at $6 per month.

> Video

Justin.tv
http://www.justin.tv
Broadcast live to the Internet from your computer's webcam.

Qik
http://www.qik.com
Enables live video broadcasting to your site, using certain types of mobile phones from Nokia, Apple, BlackBerry, and others.

TubeMogul
http://www.tubemogul.com
Upload videos to multiple sites (YouTube, Metacafe, Vimeo, etc.) simultaneously, and analyze where they're being watched most.

Skype
http://www.skype.com
Great tool for having person-to-person audio and video chats with anyone, anywhere in the world, for free. Very useful for collaboration. Some artists have also used Skype and iChat (free video chat software for Macs only) to do "virtual speaking tours," visiting with college classes or book groups over the Internet.

YouTube
http://www.youtube.com
http://www.google.com/support/youtube/bin/answer.py?answer=55754&ctx=sibling
http://www.google.com/support/youtube/bin/answer.py?answer=57389&cbid=18ero3lcm66fx&src=cb&lev=answer
Everyone knows that YouTube is the primary place where viewers watch, rate, and comment on Internet videos. But if you are an artist, you should have a special YouTube account that lets you add your logo onto your YouTube profile page, create links to your own Web site, and upload longer videos. There are specific, special YouTube accounts for directors, musicians, and comedians. See links above for instructions on how to create or upgrade to these types of accounts.

> Surveys

SurveyMonkey
http://www.surveymonkey.com
Allows you to create Web-based surveys, and analyze results. Free version can collect up to 100 responses per survey; paid version starts at $19.95 per month.

Zoomerang
http://www.zoomerang.com

Allows you to create Web-based surveys, and analyze results. Free version can collect up to 100 responses per survey; paid version starts at $19 per month.

> Membership/Subscription Management

Net Member Services
http://www.netmemberservices.com/
Membership management for Web sites. Set-up fee of $99 includes installation of software; recurring monthly fee starts at $39.95 per month.

Password Protector
http://www.passwordprotectorsd.com
Allows you to manage "protected" areas on your site for subscribers only. Pricing starts at $179, which includes installation of the software on your Web server.

Subhub
http://www.subhub.com
Complete Web publishing and content management system, which includes members-only access. Supports audio and video streaming. Starts at $97 per month.

> E-mail & Text Messaging

Constant Contact
http://www.constantcontact.com
Build and manage an e-mail list, and send out mass e-mail messages. Monthly pricing starts at $15.

iContact
www.icontact.com
Build and manage an e-mail list, and send out mass e-mail messages. Monthly pricing starts at $9.95.

Trumpia
http://www.trumpia.com/main/main_promoters.php

Collect phone numbers from fans and then communicate with them via text messages. Plans start at $10 per month.

USA Bulk SMS
http://usa.bulksms.com/w/pricing.htm
Collect phone numbers from fans and then communicate with them via text messages. A block of 200 messages credits (to send 200 texts) costs $10.60.

Vertical Response
http://www.verticalresponse.com
Build and manage an e-mail list, and send out mass e-mail messages. Monthly pricing starts at $10, but company's pay-as-you-go option can be cheaper if you send out infrequent e-mails to a smallish list.

> Funding & Donations

ArtistShare
http://www.artistshare.com/home/getting_started.aspx
Tools to help musicians build a loyal following by offering access to exclusive content. Musicians can also tap into "fan funding" for recording projects. In return, fans may get album credits, VIP concert tickets, or music lessons from the artist. ArtistShare is selective about the artists they work with. $595 initiation fee, plus monthly fees that start at $12.95.

Fundable
http://www.fundable.com
Raise money online for any sort of project. If your fund-raising goal isn't met, no one pays. Fundable passes along the money via a check or PayPal.

IndieGoGo
http://www.indiegogo.com
Post an overview of your film project to raise money for it (some information, like the screenplay, budget, or casting options, can be protected by a password). A few projects on the site have raised north of $20,000, though it's unclear how much of this came from random people who wanted to support the project versus people the filmmaker already knew simply donating money via the Web site. All funding is considered a donation, rather than an investment that will be repaid. But filmmakers

can offer credits in the film, special editions of the DVD, and other perks to donors.

PayPal Donations
https://www.paypal.com/cgi-bin/webscr?cmd=p/xcl/rec/donate-intro-outside
Accept tips and donations via PayPal, a commonly-used payment system. Fees vary. Payments that come directly from a tipper's PayPal account may be free; for others, PayPal may take as much as 4.9 percent plus 30 cents from each donation or tip.

ScratchBack
http://www.scratchback.com/
Collect tips through your site, and allow readers to get a link or "thank you" credit on your site in return. ScratchBack keeps 10 percent of all tips.

TipJoy
http://www.tipjoy.com
Collect tips through your Web site, or via e-mail or Twitter messages. TipJoy keeps 10 to 15 percent of the money you collect. (TipJoy's share drops the more money you collect.)

> Advertising

Facebook Ads
http://www.facebook.com/advertising/
Allows you to buy advertising for your latest product or event in very small increments (as little as $1 per day), targeting Facebook users by location, age, sex, or keywords (like users who've expressed an affection for U2).

Google AdWords
https://adwords.google.com
Allows you to buy advertising on Google and its many partner sites. Ads can be targeted to people searching for a particular keyword or set of keywords (like "Civil War novels") or based on the user's location. You'll pay for ads based on how many times users click on them (as little as a penny per click), but the rates for popular keywords can get pricey – sometimes into the dollars. Google allows you to put a cap on the amount you want to spend per day, or per click.

Supplemental Reading

"1,000 True Fans," by Kevin Kelly
http://www.kk.org/thetechnium/archives/2008/03/1000_true_fans.php

Kelly defines a "true fan" as someone who will purchase anything and everything you produce, and argues that creators need the support of only 1,000 of them to make a living.

"The Case Against 1,000 True Fans," by Kevin Kelly
http://www.kk.org/thetechnium/archives/2008/04/the_case_agains.php

Kelly explores some of the challenges to his theory.

"The Reality of Depending on True Fans," by Kevin Kelly
http://www.kk.org/thetechnium/archives/2008/04/the_reality_of.php

Musician Robert Rich shares with Kelly his experiences selling music and playing shows for his online fan base.

The Workbook Project, edited by Lance Weiler
http://workbookproject.com

Filmmaker Lance Weiler, along with several collaborators, tracks the new strategies and technologies changing the way movies get made – with occasional forays into music and other art forms. Lots of audio and video.

"How I Did It," by Jonathan Coulton
http://www.jonathancoulton.com/2007/05/18/how-i-did-it

Singer-songwriter Coulton talks about how he launched his career as a full-time musician, leaving behind a safe job as a computer programmer.

Jonathan Coulton Answers Your Questions

http://freakonomics.blogs.nytimes.com/2007/11/20/jonathan-coulton-answers-your-questions/

A 2007 Q&A with Coulton, covering mainstream media exposure versus blog exposure; his work writing a theme song for the videogame "Portal"; and "pay what you want" downloads.

"Blend of old, new media launched OK Go"

http://www.usatoday.com/tech/news/2006-11-27-ok-go_x.htm

USA Today story about OK Go's YouTube success.

The Long Tail and The Long Tail blog, by Chris Anderson

http://longtail.typepad.com/

What do people buy in a world of unlimited shelf space? Anderson, the editor of *Wired*, explores the universe of content that never becomes a blockbuster hit. His blog also includes posts about his 2009 book, *Free*.

"Free! Why $0.00 is the Future of Business," by Chris Anderson

http://www.wired.com/techbiz/it/magazine/16-03/ff_free

Wired Magazine cover story by Anderson exploring the idea that you can make money by giving things away – what Anderson has dubbed "freeconomics."

"Better Than Free," by Kevin Kelly

http://www.kk.org/thetechnium/archives/2008/01/better_than_fre.php

The Internet makes it very easy to copy any kind of digital file. Therefore, Kelly writes, artists "need to sell things which can't be copied." This post explores eight possibilities.

Here Comes Everybody, by Clay Shirky

Shirky's 2008 book delves into the Internet's power as an enabler of publishing, participation, and collaboration.

"Improving Your Web Site for Higher Google Rankings"

http://webdesign.about.com/cs/promotion/a/aaaagoogle.htm

"Webmaster Guidelines"
http://www.google.com/support/webmasters/bin/answer.py?answer=3576
9

Advice directly from Google about building a Web site that will show up prominently on the search engine.

How to Make Webcomics, by Scott Kurtz, Kris Straub, Dave Kellett, and Brad Gulgar

Nuts-and-bolts guide to creating a comic strip, and building a business model around it. Published in 2008, many of the ideas in this book will be relevant to other kinds of artists and writers.

YouTube: An Insider's Guide to Climbing the Charts, by Alan Lastufka and Michael W. Dean

Published in November 2008, this offers a detailed look at creating videos for YouTube and getting people to watch them.

ITVS Digital Initiative: A Report from the Field
http://www.itvs.org/producers/digitalinitiative/fieldreport

In 2008, I interviewed a group of documentary filmmakers who have been experimenting in three areas: opening up their production process; building an audience online; and exploring new distribution avenues.

Pollinate: How to Build an Audience and Keep It
http://audience.workbookproject.com

An online collection of advice, case studies, and video about cultivating an audience... mostly geared to film and video creators.

The Indie Band Survival Guide
http://www.indieguide.com

Web site and book that covers everything from publicity and CD manufacturing to tour booking. Written by the Chicago band Beatnik Turtle.

Acknowledgments

I owe a big debt to all of the artists who took time to share their advice and experiences with me, including many who don't appear in these pages. Filmmakers Lance Weiler, Tiffany Shlain, Hunter Weeks, Robert Bahar, Brian Chirls, Scott Macaulay, and Arin Crumley have been incredibly helpful, as has distribution guru Peter Broderick of Paradigm Consulting.

In 2008, Sally Jo Fifer, Jim Sommers, and Matthew Meschery at ITVS commissioned me to do a series of case studies focusing on documentary filmmakers building audiences and distributing their work in new ways, which enabled me to gather lots of great stories from the "front lines." I'm grateful for their support

Shayne Gilbert, Alyssa Stern, Ken Goldberg, and many others helped put together the first edition of The Conversation, an event held at the University of California at Berkeley in the fall of 2008, where a group of very smart folks discussed some of these issues.

I'm glad that the designer Matt W. Moore was willing to take on the job of creating the cover for this book, on a tight deadline.

On every project, including this one, I get an assist from the readers of my blog CinemaTech – and here they were especially helpful, commenting on early ideas and suggesting people to interview.

Finally, my deepest thanks to my wife Amy, my son Max, and the rest of my family, who've been incredibly supportive as I've been working on this project.

About the Author

Scott Kirsner is a journalist and blogger who writes about new ideas and their impact on the world. He edits the blog CinemaTech (http://cinematech.blogspot.com), which explores the way technology is changing the entertainment industry. He is the author of *Inventing the Movies*, a technological history of Hollywood published in 2008, and *The Future of Web Video: New Opportunities for Producers, Entrepreneurs, Media Companies and Advertisers*, first published in 2006.

He writes regularly for *Variety* and the Boston *Globe*. Scott's writing has also appeared in the New York *Times*, *The Hollywood Reporter*, *Wired*, *Fast Company*, the Los Angeles *Times*, the San Francisco *Chronicle*, *BusinessWeek*, and *Newsweek*, among other publications.

Scott is one of the founders of the Nantucket Conference on Entrepreneurship and Innovation, held each May. He also speaks and moderates regularly at entertainment industry events, including the Sundance Film Festival, the Toronto International Film Festival, and the South by Southwest Film Festival.

Scott is a graduate of Boston University's College of Communications and the New World School of the Arts, in Miami. He can be reached at kirsner@pobox.com.

The Web Site

The *Fans, Friends & Followers* Web site offers bonus interviews not included here; audio and video content; a list of events and workshops related to the book; and a chance to share your own advice on tools and strategies that have been helpful to you. Come visit!

http://www.scottkirsner.com/fff

5346237R0

Made in the USA
Lexington, KY
01 May 2010